TARGET FIELD
The New Home of the Minnesota Twins

STEVE BERG   FOREWORD BY GARRISON KEILLOR   AFTERWORD BY JOE MAUER

MVP
BOOKS

First published in 2010 by MVP Books, an imprint of MBI Publishing
Company and the Quayside Publishing Group, 400 First Avenue North,
Suite 300, Minneapolis, MN 55401 USA

MVP Books titles are also available at discounts in bulk quantity for
industrial or sales-promotional use. For details write to Special Sales
Manager at MBI Publishing Company, 400 First Avenue North, Suite
300, Minneapolis, MN 55401 USA.

To find out more about our books, visit us online at
www.mvpbooks.com.

ISBN-13: 978-0-7603-3965-7

Library of Congress Cataloging-in-Publication Data

Berg, Steve.
  Target field : the new home of the Minnesota Twins / Steve Berg ;
foreword by Garrison Keillor ; afterword by Joe Mauer.
    p. cm.
  ISBN 978-0-7603-3965-7 (hb w/ jkt)
  1. Target Field (Minneapolis, Minn.) 2. Minnesota Twins (Baseball
team) 3. Baseball fields--Minnesota--Minneapolis. I. Title.
  GV416.T37B47 2010
  796.06'8776579--dc22
                    2010023054

Editor: Josh Leventhal
Design manager: Katie Sonmor
Cover designer: John Barnett/4 Eyes Design
Book designer: Cindy Samargia Laun

Printed in China

CONTENTS

PREFACE

A Letter from the Pohlad Family

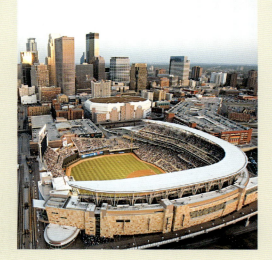

DEAR BASEBALL FANS,

In May 2007, the first shovel went into the ground to begin construction of Target Field, bringing outdoor baseball back to Minnesota. This ballpark reflects the hard work of many and is an accomplishment of which the entire community can be proud.

With the support of many community partners along the way, legislation was passed to fund the new ballpark, which began the 60-month process of planning and construction to ensure the park reflected the best of Minnesota. Finally, with tens of thousands of fans on hand on April 12, 2010, we celebrated the opening of this special park that provides the best in outdoor baseball for Minnesota fans and players alike—rain or shine.

We are excited and proud of this unique new ballpark, and we hope you are, too! This book provides an inside look at the incredible journey that began with detailed plans by seasoned architects, was nurtured by skilled craftsmen who laid its Mankato limestone cornerstone, and finally, was finished by the expert landscapers who planted the native plants and greenery that surround it.

Beyond the beauty and craftsmanship that went into it, Target Field is a truly special facility because of the game of baseball and what it represents—it has a unique way of bringing people together. The game itself creates lifelong memories: families and friends coming together as a community to root for the home team, collectively celebrating the successes, and sometimes enduring the disappointments. Fans of all ages and from all walks of life can enjoy this game of strategy, talent, and teamwork. And now, in this new ballpark, Twins fans will be able to experience outdoor baseball once again, as many believe it was meant to be played.

It took a community to build this ballpark; the list is long, but we would like to offer our sincere and heartfelt thanks to all who contributed to making Target Field a reality. First and foremost, we want to thank all of you, the Minnesota Twins fans, for your support. We also want to thank Jerry Bell of the Twins for his leadership and devoted oversight of the project, and the Hennepin County leaders and other supporters who partnered with us to make this a reality. Finally and importantly, we want to thank all of the hard-working Minnesotans who built the ballpark in record time and ahead of schedule.

As did our parents, Carl and Eloise Pohlad, we recognize both the honor and the responsibility that ownership brings. The Minnesota Twins have long been part of the fabric of this community. As we begin this first season outdoors, we look forward to even more fun and exciting experiences and memories for all of you and future generations of Minnesota baseball fans.

Go Twins!

Sincerely,

Jim Pohlad   Bob Pohlad   Bill Pohlad

Donna, Jim, Becky, Bob, Bill, Oliver, and Michelle Pohlad, at the Twins opener at Target Field on April 12, 2010.

FOREWORD
by Garrison Keillor

IT GETS COLD IN MINNESOTA AND STAYS COLD FOR LONG MONTHS when snow drifts against the outfield fence and icicles hang from the dugout roof, and this makes baseball feel all the more miraculous here in the north. The home opener in April feels like recovery from a serious illness, and on through the spring and into summer, the Minnesota fan is sometimes stunned by the simple fact of baseball's *existence*—here it is, the home team standing on the dugout steps, about to take the field, and the four gentlemen in black take their stations—after the long dark tunnel of winter on the frozen tundra, here we are in the bleachers, in the sun, and Hey! we have survived nature's attempt to kill us and we are actually *sitting outdoors* and watching men play *beisbol, mi amor.*

Here in the northern latitudes, our backs to Canada, we're naturally romantic about the game, and that's why we're such tolerant fans. We don't boo our team, we aren't demented or demanding or cranky. Outsiders think we're indifferent, but it's not true: it's just that we're so very very happy to be looking at green grass.

And so a person my age has warm aromatic memories of that old rattletrap Nicollet Park with its Spanish castle entrance where the Minneapolis Millers played the St. Paul Saints. My hero was the slugging right fielder Clint "The Hondo Hurricane" Hartung, until it became clear that he couldn't hit a curveball and that was why he'd been dropped by the Giants. And then one day, I watched him trot out to his position, stop, and casually blow his nose onto the ground, first the left nostril, then the right, and wipe his nose on his sleeve. So much for heroes: you don't want to watch too closely or they will let you down big time. The Millers moved to Met Stadium in the cornfields of Bloomington in 1956 and became a Red Sox farm club and that was how I got to see the Sox play an exhibition game against the Millers one summer night and Ted Williams come up as a pinch hitter in the late innings and show us that classic swing and poke one over the left-field fence and lope around the bases. We cheered and cheered, and he disappeared into the dugout and then (I may be wrong about this) emerged and tipped his hat.

The Washington Senators moved into the Met and became the Twins, and we flocked to see Camilo and Pedro and Zoilo and the immortal Harmon, and out beyond right field, Holsteins grazing in a pasture. The organist sat in a booth near the press box where Herb Carneal did play-by-play for WCCO, his Virginia drawl becoming part of Minnesota summer along with the screened porch and the smell of beer and honeysuckle. Over at Delta Field at the U, you could see Dave Winfield stroke home runs and pitch for the Gophers, a St. Paul boy who was destined for great things. There was usually a game at Parade Stadium on Lyndale or Midway in St. Paul, but the best was a summer night in the third deck of Metropolitan Stadium and the smell of cigar smoke and steak sandwiches and the Minnesota River off to the south.

From 1896 to 1955, fans flocked to Nicollet Park to watch the Minneapolis Millers of the American Association.

Old-time players and fans alike have fond memories of the Old Met, where they saw many ups and downs over the course of 20 seasons at Metropolitan Stadium.

Opposite: Justin Morneau and the rest of the Twins prepare to take the field for the first outdoor Major League Baseball game in Minnesota in nearly three decades.

Twins baseball played on green grass and under sunny skies was enthusiastically welcomed when Target Field debuted in April 2010.

For the generations of fans who never before experienced outdoor baseball in Minnesota, a first visit to Target Field is simply awe-inspiring.

Let it be said here and now that the Minnesota fans accommodated themselves very well to the Metrodome. We walked in and thought, "Well, this is interesting." It wasn't our choice to move the Twins indoors under a canvas sky, but we shut up about it and went and sat in it, and when the team won the Series in 1987, then nothing more was said about the place except by out-of-towners, and the more they disparaged the Dome—the weird plastic drapes in right and center, the sheer racket, the bad bounces, and the famous Pop Fly That Went Up And Never Came Down incident—the more we came to appreciate the place, the fine hecklers in the upper deck in right field, the crush in the concourse, the exit after the game and the big whoosh of air pressure that pushed you through the revolving doors.

Time moves on. Little kids come to Target Field who will not remember that anything preceded it. The past drifts away like smoke from a fire. And the glory of baseball is its continuity, from our great-grandfather's day to our grandchildren's, a long swoop of history. It is purely beautiful to see our kids grow up to love this glorious game that we've loved since childhood—to jump up at the crack of the bat and watch the arc of the ball and the dash of the outfielder, to feel the drama of the pitching duel, to be astonished over and over by the perfect tempo of the double play, to pump your right arm when the opposing slugger whiffs on the change-up for the third strike that kills the ninth-inning rally.

The summer after the Twins left Met Stadium, I drove out Cedar Avenue on a Sunday afternoon and pulled into the vast parking lot and walked around the mountains of wreckage where the grandstand had stood, and I slipped through the security fence and onto the field, which was in good shape except for bulldozer tracks in the infield. The left-field stands and bullpen and scoreboard and the flagpole were intact. I walked across the outfield. There wasn't another soul on the premises, just me and the grackles. I felt like an archeologist at the ruins of an ancient city, except it was a city I had visited often back in its glory years. I was there. I saw the great Jim Kaat stride out to the mound. I saw Tony Oliva stretch singles into doubles. I saw Rod Carew steal home base. I had trudged up those ramps with my Uncle Don and cousin Bruce and taken our seats in the third deck like birds on a wire, and now the wire had been cut.

I couldn't imagine that we'd get a new ballpark and I never imagined getting one as perfect as Target Field, but here it is, squotched in tight between the railyards and the parking ramps, with the transit trains rolling up to the left-field entrance and the towers of downtown Minneapolis rising up beyond the outfield, a great city ballpark in the class of Wrigley and Fenway and Tiger Stadium. All of our baseball ghosts can come to rest here in this exaltation of a ballpark, this astonishment on Fifth Street. Every year we will rise up from our torpors and revive ourselves with a hot dog and mustard and fresh air and be transfixed by what we've loved since we were kids. When the game starts, time stops, and we're all young again, it's spring, and the sun is shining.

When the game starts, time stops, and we're all young again,

it's spring, and the **sun** is shining.

EVERY DAY IS A GOOD DAY AT THE BALLPARK

by Steve Berg

IN SOME SENSE THE WRITING OF THIS BOOK BEGAN 50 YEARS AGO, the first time I stepped into a major league ballpark and into the grip of a lifelong enchantment. It was on a Saturday in late August 1961. The Twins were slouching toward a seventh-place finish, 38 games behind the Mantle-Maris juggernaut in New York. But Minnesota fans were taking the longer view. This was the team's first season in the Land of 10,000 Lakes. And as my dad might have told us kids as we navigated the vast Met Stadium parking lot: Every day is a good day at the ballpark.

My magic moment came after we memorized the location of our car, secured our tickets, heard the beckoning sounds of the organ and smelled the concession stand smells, threaded our way through the crowds and up the darkened ramp into the light, and in a flash, there it was! The most incredible sight a kid could imagine.

A sun-dappled carpet of grass, greener than any I'd ever seen. The Twins, high-spirited in their home pinstripes, tossing balls back and forth. They were all there! The stocky Killebrew. Allison with his pant legs pulled high. Lenny Green, smiling, his cap cocked back on his head. And over by the third-base dugout, the Baltimore Orioles in their snappy road grays with the bright orange trim, an up-and-coming bunch that featured my favorite player, the slick-fielding third baseman Brooks Robinson.

Many times I had seen these players on our black-and-white Philco, but never in color! And never with the live sounds of popping mitts and cracking bats, never with the view of the triple-decked grandstand over my shoulder, never with the melodic cries of "Hamm's beer here!" and "Getch'yer hot dogs!" filling the air. I was in my element. My life had taken a turn for the better, and I wasn't letting go.

The Twins lost that day, and the next day, too, in the drizzle, when Baltimore's 22-year-old right-hander Milt Pappas tossed a two-hit shutout and smacked a pair of home runs. But it didn't matter. From then on, the ballpark was where I wanted to be.

My story is far from unique; thousands of Twins fans share similar memories. The opening of Target Field gives us all a chance at reliving our magic moments. We are home at last!

But it didn't come easy.

Minnesotans argued for a decade about the propriety of helping the team build a new stadium. People on both sides got hot under the collar as they realized that the question was not just about baseball but about what kind of community we wanted to be. Did we really need professional sports and all the other competitive investments tugging at our pocketbooks? As the fight wore on, stadium opponents from both parties tapped into Minnesota's most potent political and cultural sensibilities, especially the populist notion that Norwegians call *janteloven*, which translates as a disdain for excessive pride or ambition or for anything fancy or showy. In the stadium debate, it meant that we would be better off without major league baseball.

A more pragmatic view eventually prevailed. Hennepin County board chairman Mike Opat got to the heart of the matter when he asked himself whether life in the Upper Midwest would be better with or without the Twins. To him the answer was obvious, so he risked his political career to lead the effort to build a new ballpark.

Designing the ballpark was another challenge. Twins executives reminded themselves again and again that this was a once-in-a-lifetime opportunity—they had one chance to get it right. Architects designed an uncommonly graceful building that reflects Minnesota's distinctive natural features, especially its craggy stone outcroppings and glassy ice crystals. It's a building attuned to the personality of Minnesotans. The structure is modest in size and doesn't lord over its surroundings. It fits seamlessly into the life of the city. Indeed, its customized fit, its elegant contemporary lines, its intimate links to transportation, and its other eco-friendly features make Target Field the most significant baseball stadium since Baltimore's Camden Yards, built in 1992.

Constructing the ballpark was a heroic feat. The site was tight and hemmed in on all sides. The building had to squeeze below some neighboring structures and over the top of others. Lack of space required contractors to build the stadium from the inside out and to follow a sequence that required extraordinary logistics and precision. Weather conditions were often brutal. Yet the project was finished on budget and two months ahead of schedule thanks to a dedicated and diverse work force. Altogether, more than 3,000 men and women, nearly all of them from Minnesota, worked on site, with thousands more from across the country contributing specialized talents and skills.

In the end, Hennepin County and the Twins delivered an extraordinary asset for the Twin Cities and the Upper Midwest. Target Field is a fun place to be. Admired by fans from around the country, it impresses even baseball agnostics, who see the structure as artful enough to be included among the city's finest architectural attractions.

Sometimes at the new ballpark I close my eyes and let my childhood sensations come rushing back in. As I write this, my dad is in his 90s and in failing health. My dream is to take him to Target Field, sit side by side in the sunshine, rekindle the memories of that first day we sat at the Old Met watching the new Twins, and remind him of the words he said that day: Every day is a good day at the ballpark.

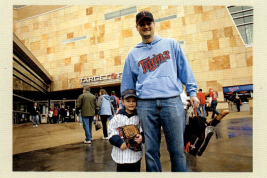

It's never a bad day at the ballpark when you can share the moment with family, friends, and community.

More than just a place to play baseball, Target Field is an artful addition to the Minneapolis skyline and provides a new family attraction to its downtown neighborhood.

1

PLAY BALL!

Opening Day

"I keep looking around **amazed** that this is our ballpark."

—*Justin Morneau, first baseman, Minnesota Twins*

othing lifts the spirit like an early spring. To shed the big coat weeks sooner than expected, to stroll down the street in shirtsleeves, to savor the sun's warmth on your neck, to smell fresh grass and feel the nearness of baseball's arrival is a gift almost too intoxicating to handle. Then to realize that today is the day that the Minnesota Twins, after 28 years, return to playing home games under nature's open sky and on nature's real grass—well, all that's enough to make a person downright giddy.

It explains the dreamy mood on the streets and sidewalks leading to spanking-new Target Field on this extraordinary April morning in 2010. The trains are running full. Clumps of people in all variety of Twins jerseys and caps walk briskly through downtown, heads tilted forward in anticipation. The pace slows as the crowds thicken near the ballpark. It's five hours until game time, but already the plaza is filling up. Pessimists predict rain, but sunglasses outnumber umbrellas five to one.

Del Hager has driven five hours from Grand Forks with hopes of somehow finding a ticket. He brims with childhood memories of trips to old Met Stadium in his family's rusty camper. Jerry Holby from Minneapolis sits on a bench reminiscing about his grandfather's devotion to outdoor baseball. "We buried him with his Twins cap," he says. "If only he could have seen *this!*"

This has become a kind of baseball love-in. No one has painted his or her face for war—only for pure fun. The crowd is smiley and polite, discovering all kinds of treasures and memories on the plaza and standing on tiptoes to catch a glimpse of the Kirby Puckett statue now being unveiled.

A bespectacled man in the midst of the throng goes unrecognized, but he is Mike Opat, the Hennepin County commissioner who, perhaps more than anyone, is responsible for turning this dream into reality. In four hours, he will toss out a ceremonial first pitch, but for now he's content to mingle and absorb the smiling faces. "This makes it all worthwhile," he says.

At noon, the gates swing open and people spill into the park itself. A whole generation has never seen the Twins play a home game outdoors, let alone in a beauty of a ballpark like this. "This is ours?!?" a young woman shrieks into her cell phone. "It's awesome! Where are you? We're at Gate 34. Come find us!"

Amid the whoops and hollers, Stewart and Julie Lewis snap photos of one another. Their tickets are a gift from their three children back in Spencer, Iowa. "It's the best present we could imagine," Julie says.

Not far away someone spills a cup of beer and a boisterous observance marks the spot. "The first error!" somebody cries. "Don't tell Gardy!"

People explore eagerly. "I'm just gob-smacked!" says Mary Milla of Minneapolis as she checks out the Legends Club. Dan Oberdorfer, who lives a few blocks from the park, says, "This is first class. We're used to doing things on the cheap in Minnesota, but this is as good as anybody else's. Maybe better."

"I'm proud to be a Minnesotan," says Graydon Royce, the *Star Tribune*'s theater critic. Now people won't be ashamed to take out-of-town visitors to a ballgame, he muses. "In the Dome, we were like the lady with 14 cats. Nobody really wanted to come over."

Target Field brims with excitement on April 12, 2010, as Twins fans anticipate their first outdoor home game in nearly three decades.

Above: An empty ballpark on April 11, 2010

Right: Grounds crew members work hard to prepare the field for the ballpark's debut. They paint the lines, groom the dirt, and tend the grass—as they will for all 81 home dates.

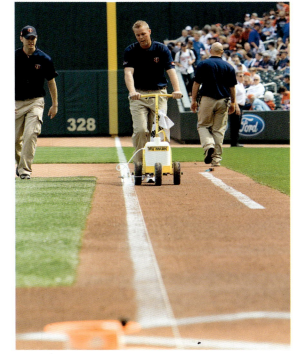

Now, even before the first pitch, it's clear that Target Field is lifting Twins fans to a higher level. They feel authentic. "We're back in the big leagues," is how Mitch Forderer puts it, recalling road trips to outdoor baseball games across the country. Now, finally, those road trips can happen at home, he says.

It's a theme that players talk about, too. They feel validated. Down on the sun-dappled field, with his teammates taking batting practice, Nick Punto says, "It's just breathtaking. They didn't cut any corners. This is as good as it gets. It truly feels like the big leagues."

Jim Thome, the strapping veteran who signed with the Twins over the winter, launches a fat pitch onto the plaza, then strides toward the dugout talking about his gratitude for getting to help open three new parks—in Cleveland in 1994, in Philadelphia in 2004, and now this one. "Being a part of all that, that's really neat," he says.

Over on the steps of the Red Sox dugout, Terry Francona, the Boston manager, pauses to stuff tobacco into his mouth. "Gorgeous, just gorgeous," he manages to say as he peers out over the sunny green grass and into the looming city skyline. "I'm happy for the Twins." A few steps away, David Ortiz, the Boston slugger and former Twin, laughs about getting lost on the way to the new park. "We were headed toward Minnetonka," he says, shaking his head. "Fourteen years ago when I came here they were talking about this," he says, gazing into the outfield. "It reminds me a little of Cleveland, a little of Seattle, a little of Pittsburgh—the best of everything."

As game time approaches, broadcasters Joe Castiglione and Dave O'Brien describe the new digs to the Red Sox radio nation. "The Twins are going to be sky high," O'Brien warns. "There's so much buzz going down today in the city of Minneapolis. You see Twins gear everywhere, even people working in the offices downtown here are all decked out in their Joe Mauer jerseys."

The opening ceremonies are enough to leave grown men misty-eyed. The team, wearing vintage-style uniforms from 1961, is introduced to thunderous applause. A giant flag is unfurled, gospel choirs sing, fireworks explode, four F-16s roar low over the field. And umpire Jeff Nelson, one of three Twin Cities natives on today's crew, chants the words that people have been waiting so long to hear outdoors: "Play ball!"

The game unfolds this way: Marco Scutaro, the Boston leadoff man, gets the first hit in the new park, a line single to center. Minnesota's Denard Span scores the first run, and the Twins take the lead. Joe Mauer finishes the day with three base hits. Jason Kubel smacks the ballpark's first home run, a shot into the right field Overlook in the seventh inning. The Twins win 5–2 behind Carl Pavano, who gives up only four hits in six innings.

To hear the ESPN crew tell it, the new ballpark is the biggest winner. "So much character," Chris Singleton keeps saying. "A beautiful place to behold." Isn't it ironic, he wonders, that "only ten years ago this franchise was marked for contraction?"

Ironic, yes, but more than that. Target Field, with all of its sensual architecture and the glorious baseball environment, is the destination on a long journey from heartache to joy, a trip from near-death to new life.

"I'm like a **little kid** in a candy store."

—*Nick Punto, infielder, Minnesota Twins*

Top: Tons of people arrive early to watch batting practice and pre-game warmups.

Bottom: Even food service folks huddle up for a pre-game strategy session. Everything must be in order to satisfy the nearly 40,000 customers about to storm the gates.

Above: People gather on Target Plaza hours before game time to partake in the communal and celebratory atmosphere of Opening Day.

Right: Shortly before noon on April 12, 2010, Kirby Puckett Jr. is the first fan through the turnstiles. He enters through Gate 34, named after his late father's number.

Opposite top: Spectators quickly fill the concourses and escalators, eager to find their seats and explore their new baseball home.

Opposite bottom: Some fans can't contain their enthusiasm, as they wave commemorative homer hankies and catch a first glimpse of the new ballpark's interior.

"When I was 13, my dad took me to the old Met.

We're starting a **new tradition** today."

—Dave Johnson, Stillwater, Minnesota

"**Wow!** This is way more

than I ever dreamed."

—Travis Johnson, age 13,
Stillwater, Minnesota,
stepping into Target Field
with his dad for the first time

The Twins wear vintage-styled 1961 uniforms for the game, honoring the 50th season of major league baseball in Minnesota.

Ceremonial first pitches are thrown by three key figures in the ballpark project. Dave Mansell, general superintendent for Mortenson Construction, delivered the first first pitch, followed by Hennepin County Commissioner Mike Opat (left), who championed the legislative backing for Target Field. The final ceremonial pitch is delivered by Jerry Bell, president of Twins Sports Inc. (right), who led the team's drive for a stadium for over a decade. All-time Twins legends Tony Oliva, Kent Hrbek, Rod Carew, and Harmon Killebrew and Kirby Puckett Jr.—representing the team's five retired numbers—brought out the ceremonial balls from center field.

An enormous replica of Old Glory, nearly filling the outfield, is unfurled by about 150 representatives of Mortenson Construction and others who participated in the ballpark project.

A combined chorus—including The Steeles, The Sounds of Blackness, Moore by Four, and the Twin Cities Community Gospel Ensemble—sings the National Anthem.

Opening Day ceremonies include the raising of championship banners. The banners recall the World Series wins in 1987 and 1991; the American League pennant in 1965; and division titles in 1969, 1970, 2002, 2003, 2004, 2006, and 2009. Each flag is hoisted by a member of those teams.

"The atmosphere is great. I was distracted between every pitch. **I'm in awe...**

Pretty cool. My head was on a swivel from the minute I walked in."

—*Michael Cuddyer, right fielder, Minnesota Twins*

Opposite: The opening ceremonies' most dramatic moment comes as the National Anthem concludes, four F-16 jets fly over the ballpark, and fireworks shoot up from the scoreboard. It's a magical moment of impeccable timing and coordination.

Minnesota's Carl Pavano delivers the first pitch to Boston's leadoff hitter, Marco Scutaro, at exactly 3:13 pm on April 12, 2010.

Lineup card from the inaugural game at Target Field

Jason Kubel belts the first home run in Target Field history, a solo shot to open the seventh inning.

Fans in the Overlook section of right field anticipate Kubel's incoming home run. The ball travels 388 feet and is caught by a young fan from Lawton, Iowa.

Reigning MVP and hometown hero Joe Mauer gets off to a good start at Target Field. He went three-for-five and drove in two runs.

The imposing Jon Rauch pitches a perfect ninth inning to earn the save in Minnesota's 5–2 win.

Denard Span notches the first stolen base at Target Field in the fourth inning. Earlier, in the first inning, he scored the new ballpark's first run.

Congratulations all around. Joe Mauer and Jim Thome share a fist-bump after the historic victory over the Red Sox. The Twins go on to win six of nine games in their first home stand at Target Field.

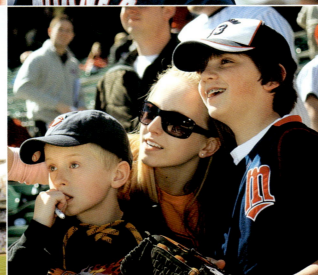

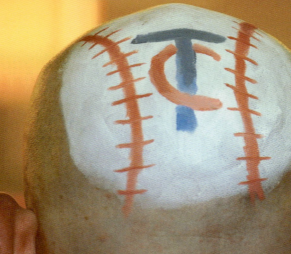

For the first time in nearly three decades, Twins fans embrace and endure all kinds of weather, from full sun to sprinkles of rain.

Fans appreciate Target Field's environmentally friendly transportation options. Hundreds ride bikes to the park. Thousands arrive by light rail, which carries nearly 20 percent of all fans attending games.

EXTRA INNINGS

Why It Took 13 Years to Build a Ballpark

"When we bought the Twins, we had no concept

of what it would mean to own a baseball team,

the **emotional involvement** of the public that went with it.

And we had no concept of the process

of what it would take to build a new stadium."

—Jim Pohlad, Minnesota Twins owner and CEO

The freeways and skyscrapers of big-city Minneapolis

"Minnesota is the only state—except maybe for Texas—where we **truly** believe that, no matter what, we're better than everybody else. And we're puzzled that other people don't see it."

—*Larry Redmond, lobbyist*

No American place endured a bumpier ride on its way to a new baseball stadium than Minneapolis–St. Paul. Between July 1994, when the Twins first made public their hope for a new ballpark, and May 2007, when construction finally began, the city and state suffered through something close to a mental breakdown. Ostensibly the issue was baseball, but really it was more than that.

The quest for a ballpark became a kind of long-running morality play through which Minnesotans posed tough questions about themselves and their place in the world. The century was turning. The global economy, as Thomas Friedman later described it, was flattening in a way that required faster running just to stay even. To spend public money—of any amount—on a baseball stadium hit a raw nerve and prompted an identity crisis of sorts: What kind of a place did we want Minnesota to be?

Did we want to keep pace with global competition? Did we want to ante up—not only for professional sports teams, but also to advance public education, green space, mass transit, the arts, bioscience research, and a slew of other prerequisites that defined the modern, successful global city?

Or did we want to jump off the treadmill and retreat to a simpler time—escape to the backyard to grill burgers, chop wood, and disengage from the mounting complexity and the mounting demands on our pocketbooks? As garage logic had it, the Twin Cities was a pretty good place—with or without baseball—and pretty good was good enough.

It wasn't an easy choice. We Minnesotans crave the national attention that comes with professional sports. We understand the benefits to our civic spirit and our quality of life. But there's another side to our personality. Our agrarian roots, our pietistic values, our fierce populism, our disdain for conspicuous wealth, our steadfast belief that Minnesota is an exceptional place that doesn't need to follow the crowd—all those traits worked against securing a new ballpark and guaranteeing the viability of major league baseball in Minnesota. For many, the idea of using public money to build a ballpark was just plain wrong—end of story. Yes, they liked, even loved, the Twins. But many people weren't interested in throwing money into a hat, even when the team seemed headed out of town or selected for extinction. The fact that more than a dozen competing cities had spent billions of dollars in public money on new stadiums didn't impress most Minnesotans.

"This fight wasn't really about politics or competitive economics," said Larry Redmond, a lobbyist who has worked the corridors of the state capitol on sports and arts issues for more than two decades. "This fight was about culture, and culture is always the hardest nut to crack."

A PLACE ON THE MAP

When the ballpark debate emerged in the mid-1990s, the Twins had been a fixture on the local scene for more than three decades. The team's arrival from Washington, D.C., in 1961 had been part of a larger civic project aimed at putting Minneapolis and St. Paul on the proverbial national map. As separate cities, they were inconspicuous Midwestern places. But joined as a unified market, they could become a national player in business, education, sports, and the arts—at least, that was the strategy.

Securing a place on the map was important in those days, especially for cities in the nation's midsection. Nonstop commercial jet travel between the coasts had begun in 1959. No land-locked city wanted to be dismissed as "flyover territory."

Baseball had anticipated the jet age by opening two big California markets to the Brooklyn Dodgers and New York Giants in 1958. Midwestern cities, too, had attracted franchises from the East. The Boston Braves had moved to Milwaukee in 1953 and the Philadelphia Athletics to Kansas City in 1955.

By 1961, it was the Twin Cities' turn. In anticipation of his move, Washington Senators owner Calvin Griffith hoped to rename his team the Twin Cities Twins—hence the "TC" logo on the team caps. When the American League rejected "Twin Cities" as a gimmick, Griffith became the  first baseball owner to name his club for a state. (Later, teams in Dallas–Fort Worth, Denver, Miami, Phoenix, and for a time, Los Angeles, assumed the names of their states.)

The Twins, and the NFL's Vikings, were the sports cogs in the wider metro strategy. Building a new airport terminal, Orchestra Hall, the Nicollet Mall, the skyways, and the Guthrie and Children's theaters; expanding the art museums; and founding the Metropolitan Council were all part of the campaign to raise the profile of the Twin Cities. When, in 1973, *Time* magazine ran a 12-page cover story celebrating Minnesota as "the state that works" and the Twin Cities as home to "the good life," the strategy was declared a success. As was later noted in the *Star Tribune*, "An improbable metropolis had risen from a cold, remote landscape and the whole country was taking notice."

Calvin Griffith arriving in Minnesota in November 1960

Metropolitan Stadium, mid-1960s

THE MET AND THE DOME

Metropolitan Stadium was built for $10.3 million by the city of Minneapolis in 1956 to attract a major league team, and it became the Twins' (and Vikings') first home in 1961. Surrounded by a vast parking lot that spread along Cedar Avenue in Bloomington, the Met reflected perfectly the style of the 1950s. Glossy multi-colored bricks gave the stadium's exterior the look of a bathroom in a mid-century ranch-style house. Seats were painted aqua. Temporary bleachers along the left field line were never made permanent. By the mid-1970s, a series of patchwork expansions had increased the ballpark's capacity to just 48,500. That small number of seats for football—and their baseball-friendly configuration—did not meet NFL requirements. The league urged the Vikings to find another home.

In fact, neither team was happy with Met Stadium's deteriorating condition. In 1982, the Twins, hoping that the great indoors would attract larger crowds on cool spring and fall days, joined the Vikings in their new football digs, the Hubert H. Humphrey Metrodome on the east end of downtown Minneapolis.

On the drawing board since the early 1970s, the Dome was built as "Minnesota's rec room." It looked the part. Legislation had capped the budget at $55 million, giving the Dome the spare, utilitarian look of a converted basement. The puffy, fiberglass roof protected football fans from Minnesota's notoriously early winters. The challenges for baseball were many.

During the inaugural season, fans sweltered and home runs flew into the seats as if shot from cannons, until air conditioning was installed in 1983. The artificial turf, especially in the early years, was so bouncy that looping fly balls hitting the floor were catapulted

METROPOLITAN STADIUM
"Home of the Minnesota Twins & Vikings"

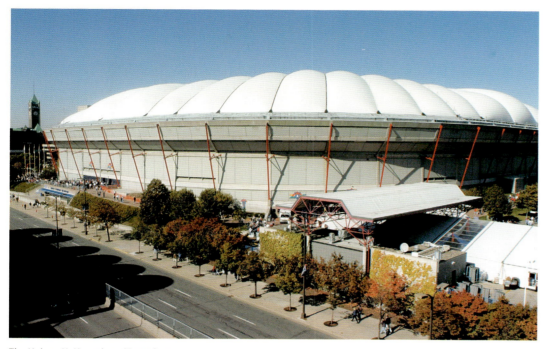

The Hubert H. Humphrey Metrodome

over the heads of charging fielders. Players often lost sight of fly balls, and for good reason: the roof was the same color as a baseball. Pop-ups occasionally caromed off loudspeakers that dangled over the field. Twice, fly balls defied Newton's law by never coming down. Oakland's Dave Kingman in 1984 and the Twins' Corey Koskie in 2004 hit towering pop-ups that lodged between the layers of fabric in the roof.

Visiting players and managers loathed the Dome. Dan Quisenberry, the legendary Kansas City reliever, said he generally opposed nuclear weapons, except in the case of the Metrodome. St. Louis Cardinals manager Whitey Herzog and Atlanta Braves skipper Bobby Cox blamed the Dome for World Series losses in 1987 and 1991, respectively. Torii Hunter, who spent nine years as the Twins' center fielder before signing with the Los Angeles Angels, said that if the Dome were ever to be blown up, he'd like to push the plunger.

Fans had problems, too. Seating rows were so long that a single fan leaving his or her seat could block the view of scores of others. The lighting was terrible. Sight lines were dreadful. Many fans had to turn their heads 80 degrees to see home plate, prompting one reviewer to remark, "Chiropractors must love this place." It was just one of many commentaries that savaged the Dome.

Of the 55,000 seats for baseball, only 6,000 could be counted as quality seats, and that's being generous. Folded-up football seats in right field gave the stadium the look of a high school gym. A huge plastic fence, also in right, became a signature feature of the Dome—the "Baggie" was hardly as artistic as the ivy-covered walls in Chicago or the fountains in Kansas City.

"[The Metrodome] wasn't a good place to play baseball, but there was great **baseball** played in that place."

—*Torii Hunter, centerfielder, Los Angeles Angels*

Right: Fans packed into the Metrodome and cheered their hearts out during the World Series in 1987.

Below: In the lean years of the mid-1990s, there were lots of empty blue seats at the Dome.

For serious baseball fans, the Dome offered no poetry, nothing to make it a great place to be, unless the Twins were on a hot streak. Yes, the place was exciting with the crowd in full roar, most often in the postseason. But baseball isn't only about winning. It's about falling in love—with the game, with a team, with a place. A successful ballpark earns lasting affection from one generation to the next, through good seasons and bad.

Aside from failing the fans, the Metrodome failed the team financially. Because Griffith's Twins were late to the table in the planning for the Dome, the Vikings grabbed most of the revenue-generating benefits that stadiums routinely produce for their tenants: suites, signs, parking, concessions, and so on. Even in years when the Twins had winning teams, the scarcity of quality seats limited the ball club's ability to sell season tickets. As a result, the Twins claimed to be losing tens of millions in the Dome every year.

Despite its flaws, the Metrodome delivered a huge bang for the buck to state government. From its opening in 1982 through 2006, the public spent $33.4 million on the building, including debt service and operations. But the Dome returned $245.6 million in tax revenues—more than seven times the original investment. Minneapolis, the city that raised taxes to build the stadium, did not benefit directly, but the state made out like gangbusters. For an original investment of zero dollars, the state made $234.2 million off the Dome during its first 24 years of operation, according to a report from RSM McGladrey.

The Metrodome produced more than money, of course. Two World Series, a Super Bowl, the NCAA men's basketball Final Four, several regional NCAA basketball tournaments, one season of Timberwolves basketball, a Rolling Stones concert, and more than 150 University of Minnesota football games all took place at the Dome, along with hundreds of community events, big and small. In the end, the Metrodome was like the suit you bought at a discount store: The material was flimsy, the fit wasn't quite right, and you never really liked it—but it was a terrific bargain.

"My life is miserable when I come in here.

The atmosphere is real **loud**, a very loud ballpark. . . .

Nobody's sad to leave this place."

—Ozzie Guillen, White Sox manager, before his last series at the Dome

THE CAMDEN YARDS EFFECT

Rarely has one piece of architecture had such a dramatic effect on the aesthetics and economics of an industry as Baltimore's Oriole Park at Camden Yards had on baseball in the early 1990s.

At the time, the game, from a business perspective, seemed bent on destroying itself. Players clamored for more money and more freedom to jump from team to team. Owners in larger markets resisted sharing revenue with owners in smaller ones. A panel of economists warned that baseball was poisoned by "money, conflict, and distrust." Unless the owners and players reinvented the league's economic structure, huge disparities would develop between big- and small-market teams.

One possible remedy for the smaller and mid-sized markets was a new kind of stadium, one that provided such a grand experience for fans that it mattered less how the team performed on the field—and also produced flusher streams of revenue for the teams themselves, giving them a better chance to compete. Camden Yards, nestled into Baltimore's historic Inner Harbor, became the prototype.

The new Baltimore ballpark was the brainchild of Mayor William Donald Schaefer. The city had been devastated when, on March 29, 1984, its beloved NFL team, the Colts, had packed up in the middle of the night and sneaked off to Indianapolis. Schaefer was furious, and he began a campaign to build a new baseball park to prevent a similar stunt by the Orioles. After the Colts misadventure, Marylanders didn't need much convincing. Within five years, construction had begun on a $234 million ballpark, nearly all of which (96 percent) was financed by the public, mostly from state lottery proceeds. Camden Yards opened on April 6, 1992.

Eutaw Street, the pedestrian thoroughfare, runs beyond the right field walls at Camden Yards.

Oriole Park at Camden Yards, Baltimore

Baseball's economics—

and its architecture—had

been **transformed**.

Fans had never seen anything like it. The place was obviously new, yet it looked and felt like a classic ballpark from baseball's early days. The Orioles' new home was meant to evoke memories of the sport's romantic past. The architects used steel columns, beams, and trusses instead of concrete pillars. A red brick façade with arched windows on the exterior, ornate light towers above the grandstand, and an ivy-covered batter's-eye produced a nostalgic feel. The adjoining B&O Railroad Warehouse, built in 1898, was restored and formed a backdrop in right field, with Eutaw Street remade as a terrace running beyond the right-field wall. From there, fans could stand and mingle and look down at the field while sipping beer and munching local crab cakes or barbecued pork sandwiches. Going to an Orioles game became an experience larger than baseball.

Designed by the Kansas City–based HOK Sport Venue Event (later renamed Populous), the ballpark did more than mix old and new. It mixed baseball with nearby hotels, restaurants, and family attractions. Museums, boat rides, the National Aquarium, and the popular Harborplace market were only steps away.

Traditional ballpark charm was packaged with modern conveniences. Escalators linked wide concourses. Team stores, concession stands, restaurants, and restrooms were everywhere. Suites and club seats were sold at premium prices, but reasonably priced seats were available, too. The scoreboard was state of the art. The city's glassy skyline loomed just above the commuter train station in center field. Nearby freeways provided easy access from up and down the Mid-Atlantic.

In the first decade of Camden Yards, attendance at Orioles games rose by 55 percent, from an average of 29,000 at the old stadium to 45,000 in the new one. The additional revenue from gate receipts, as well as luxury suites and advertising, was pumped back into the team.

An entire generation of urban, retro-style ballparks would follow as teams rushed to copy Baltimore's success. Baseball's economics—and its architecture—had been transformed. From his thirty-eighth-floor office in downtown Minneapolis, Carl Pohlad couldn't help but gaze out and wonder where a Twins version of Camden Yards might fit.

MELTDOWN AT THE CAPITOL

The success of Camden Yards posed a dilemma for the Twins. A dozen or more teams could easily explain how Baltimore's example had made their stadiums obsolete. Take the Indians, for example. Their fans could plainly see that rickety Cleveland Municipal Stadium, built in 1931 and aptly nicknamed the "Mistake by the Lake," was past its prime. But for Twin Citians, the Metrodome was still new—economically obsolete, yes, but chronologically new. The Twins were in only their thirteenth season in the Dome when Pohlad summoned the courage to announce for the first time, on July 18, 1994, that his team needed a new ballpark.

His claim didn't sit well with the public. Perhaps it was true that the Dome had been caught at the wrong end of a construction cycle. Perhaps the Dome was the last of the multipurpose stadiums, and its lack of charm and high-end amenities did leave it incapable of supporting a competitive team. But that wasn't the public's problem. That was Pohlad's problem. Wasn't he the state's second richest man? Why couldn't he just write a check for a new stadium if that's what he wanted?

The baseball players' strike—which began less than a month after Pohlad's announcement and resulted in the cancellation of the remainder of the 1994 season, including the World Series—didn't exactly garner public sympathy for investing in a stadium for what seemed like the greedy and arrogant forces on both sides of the labor dispute.

It was in this climate that the Twins brought their stadium problem to the state capitol in 1996. The effort backfired when opponents brilliantly constructed a frame for the issue, a frame that would prove nearly impossible to overcome: The question wasn't whether the Twins should have a new home but whether the public should pay even a dime of the cost.

Governor Arne Carlson, a Republican, shared the public's disgust with professional sports. The ignominious departure of the North Stars to Dallas in 1993 and the city-state bailout of Target Center two years later fueled public cynicism. That wealthy sports stars from the Vikings and Timberwolves were having run-ins with the police didn't help either.

Still, the Twins had been good citizens, and Carlson didn't want to lose baseball. He considered the state's finances healthy enough to cut a deal with Pohlad. He told his study group—the first of eight such groups that would spend a decade chewing over the stadium question—to intensify negotiations. The aim was to pass a bill in 1997.

Years later, Carlson regretted his approach. "The vision and public buy-in should have come before the financing and the politics," he said. Ideally, in Carlson's retrospective view, a major community project would have a clear vision, a distinct idea of what the ballpark would look and feel like, and where it would be located. Only then would the task of finding the money come into play. But for the Twins, a financial deal was always the first consideration. Which tax to raise (cigarettes, lottery, gambling, hotels, rental cars, tickets, sports memorabilia) was always the primary concern. The lesson of Camden Yards—that a ballpark could deliver an exceptional experience far beyond baseball—was ignored time and again.

Carl Pohlad throwing out the first pitch at the Metrodome shortly after taking over the team in 1984.

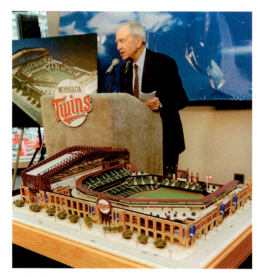

Carl Pohlad shows off the model for a proposed retractable-roof stadium for Minneapolis in January 1997.

Governor Arne Carlson expressed a "deep sense of loss" after the stadium bill failed at the legislature in November 1997. He said Minnesotans will "look back and tell our children and their children what it was like to have baseball."

A SEMANTIC BLUNDER

Governor Carlson's mission of passing a bill in 1997 began with a bang. "Twins, Carlson Deal Near" proclaimed the headline above Patrick Sweeney's scoop in the *St. Paul Pioneer Press*. Pohlad would contribute $82.5 million, about a quarter of the $350 million cost of a retractable-roof stadium to be built, most likely, on Minneapolis' historic riverfront (where the Guthrie Theater now stands). The state legislature would decide the other financial details, but no general tax revenues would be needed. Pohlad would allow the state to capture millions of dollars in naming rights and other stadium revenues that teams normally get. And, in an unprecedented gesture, he would donate 49 percent of the ball club to the state, meaning that Minnesota would get half of the windfall that would accrue from the new stadium.

The deal was a dream for Minnesota, or so it seemed. It was more generous than previous agreements in Baltimore, Cleveland, Denver, and Dallas–Fort Worth. No team had ever offered to share profits with the public.

But the details were hard to follow. "If a fourth grader can't understand it, it won't pass over here," State Representative Loren Jennings told the *Star Tribune*'s Jay Weiner. When reporters started asking tough questions, the skin began to peel away. Four days after their big announcement, the parties admitted that Pohlad's $82.5 million "contribution" wasn't a gift at all but something more like a loan. Maybe in the parlance of high finance it was a contribution or an investment that a banker like Pohlad would naturally expect to get back. But on main street Minnesota, it was a loan, plain and simple.

The Twins had committed a semantic blunder that shattered the trust between the public and the team and poisoned the debate for years. The team's allies felt especially betrayed. "It was the biggest mistake in all of the 13 years," said Jerry Bell, president of Twins Sports Inc., the man who led the team's stadium effort from beginning to end. "We were ill-advised on our response, but we have to take full responsibility because we agreed to it."

It was a classic public-relations nightmare. The Twins failed to explain that the deal was really a quid pro quo: Pohlad would advance the state $82.5 million toward a public stadium, and in return, the state would get 49 percent interest in the team. It was the best offer the state would ever get. The Twins also failed to point out that the state, not the team, had crafted the loan idea. Bell called the mistake "fatal."

At the legislative special session that November, the ballpark arrived as a patient on a gurney, wheeled in for a last-chance transfusion. Perhaps never in state history did emotion run so high on a single bill. Calls overwhelmed the Capitol's telephone system. The vote count was close at first, then fell away. The defeat was convincing. The riverfront ballpark was dead. Carlson feared the loss of Minnesota's major league franchise. "We turned our attention to other things," he said.

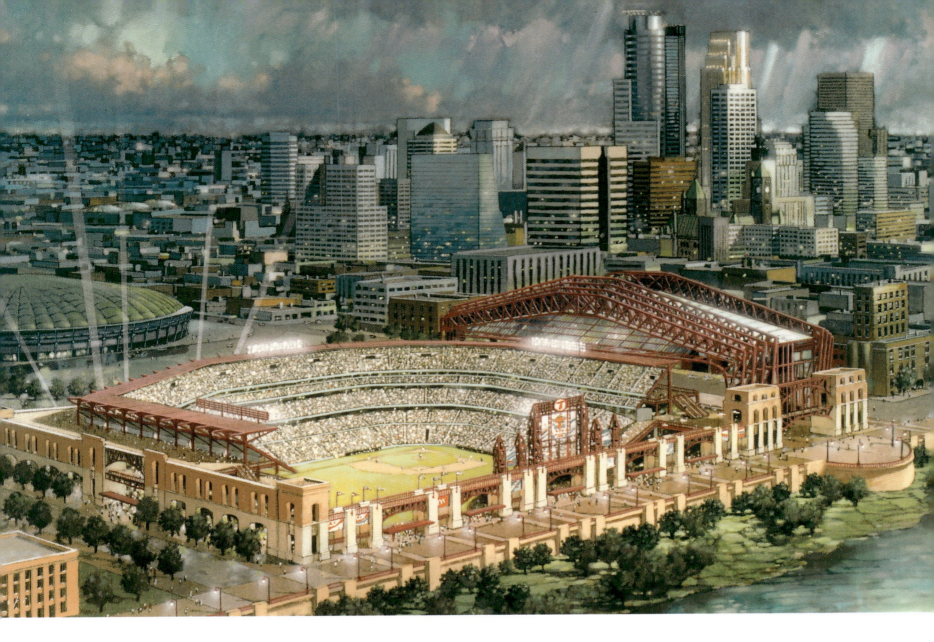

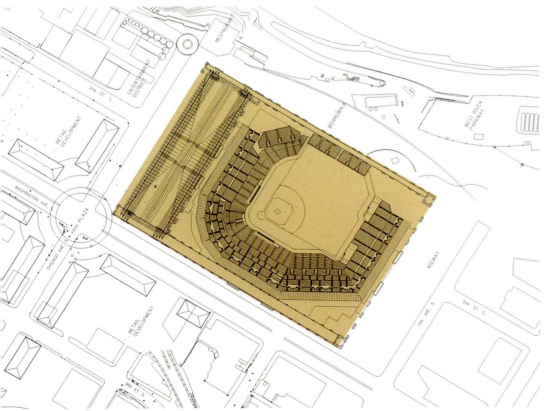

The riverfront site in downtown Minneapolis, just a few blocks north of the Metrodome, was the coveted real estate for a new Twins stadium throughout the late 1990s. With an architecture reminiscent of the Camden Yards model, the proposed ballpark was to have a retractable roof, which would be stored behind the third-base side when not in use. A riverfront promenade ran beyond the left-field wall and offered open views into the ballpark (similar to what the San Francisco Giants incorporated into AT&T Park on San Francisco Bay). The deal for the riverfront park fell apart during the legislative session of November 1997, and the site ultimately went to the new Guthrie Theater, which opened in 2006.

Don Beaver in North Carolina, 1997

"GOIN' TO CAROLINA IN MY MIND"

With the Twins' Metrodome lease expiring at the end of the 1998 season, desperation hung over the governor's office. The idea of threatening relocation was raised. After all, the White Sox had been packing for Tampa–St. Petersburg when the Illinois legislature stepped in to fully finance a new stadium on Chicago's South Side in 1988.

Carlson concedes that someone might have suggested to Twins officials in casual conversation that a similar relocation "crisis" be created. Bell also doesn't dispute that such a conversation occurred. Twins consultant Bob Starkey recalls that "from the highest level" the team was advised to find an out-of-town buyer. In any case, it was in the context of a threat to move the team that North Carolina businessman Don Beaver fell into the picture. A minority owner of the Pittsburgh Pirates, Beaver dreamed of bringing a major league team to his home state, and specifically to a suburban strip outside Greensboro, near the geographic center of the state.

In retrospect, the plan was absurd. While North Carolina had double Minnesota's population, the state's metropolitan nexus was spread thinly along a 150-mile crescent running from Raleigh through Greensboro to Charlotte. The crescent of cities lacked the critical mass needed for baseball to succeed. Only one city, Charlotte, came close to matching the size or buying power of Minneapolis–St. Paul. And, for a time, Charlotte's leading potential investor, Hugh McColl, then the chairman of Nation's Bank (later Bank of America), expressed interest in the Twins, even to the point of showing the team possible locations in downtown Charlotte.

Pohlad, nonetheless, forged an agreement to sell the Twins to Beaver if a stadium referendum passed in the Greensboro area. He also reserved the right to change his mind. "Carl changed his mind a lot," Bell said.

Greensboro voters rejected the stadium plan on May 5, 1998. Pohlad was trapped. He couldn't make money in the Twin Cities, he couldn't get a new stadium, and he couldn't move or sell his ball club. The World Series glories of 1987 and 1991 seemed very far away. The aging banker, whose life had revolved around deal-making, was finally out of options. "It was a depressing time," Bell recalled.

LOSING MAKES THINGS HARDER

On the field, the team played miserably. The 1999 season was the seventh of what would be eight straight losing seasons. Of the 30 major league clubs, the Twins were twenty-ninth in attendance, thirtieth in payroll, and thirtieth in wins. They lost 97 games and finished last in the American League Central Division, 33 games behind Cleveland. The roster was stacked with inexperienced players.

The most telling sign of the team's dire straits could be found in the meager local revenues, those produced by the Metrodome and local broadcasting contracts. Not only did those revenues rank twenty-ninth in the league, but they were astonishingly low—ten times lower than the Yankees' revenues and four times lower than the major league average. Given all that, it was easy to conclude that Pohlad's organization had given up.

For the devoted baseball follower, it was a bittersweet experience to sit in the sparse, vast blueness of the Metrodome with the echo of the game going on below. Just a few seasons earlier, the Twins had drawn three million fans. But in the late 1990s, when a foul ball rattled around in the upper deck, a fan from another section could leisurely walk over to retrieve it. When he felt the need for beer, he could walk past shuttered refreshment counters and stand first in line at a window that happened to be open. Baseball and the Twins appeared to have alienated a whole generation of fans.

Bad teams and the quest for public money were largely to blame, but the Metrodome also played a part. Its profound failure as a civic gathering place was increasingly apparent as Minnesotans traveled the country. By 2000, new-generation ballparks based on the Baltimore model stood at various stages of operation, construction, and planning in 15 cities. Most of them had been designed as part of the "experience economy," an idea conceived by Joseph Pine II and James Gilmore that the value of a ball game was about more than baseball. The new ballparks presented themselves as festival marketplaces integral to their surroundings. Going to a Giants game also meant taking a trolley and strolling along San Francisco Bay. Going to a Rockies game meant threading your way through the brewpubs of "LoDo," the historic section of Denver.

In contrast, a game at the dreary Dome meant navigating the sea of weedy parking lots that dominated the east end of downtown Minneapolis. There was no value to the experience other than to occasionally see the big-time clubs come through town to throttle the Twins. What stadium supporters most feared was that the Twins had become irrelevant to Minnesota's culture, that the Dome had erased the sensual memory of an authentic baseball experience.

What stadium supporters most feared was that the Twins had become irrelevant to Minnesota's culture, that the Dome had **erased** the sensual memory of an authentic baseball experience.

Manager Tom Kelly witnessed a lot of losing seasons at the Dome in the late 1990s.

A DESTRUCTIVE SIBLING RIVALRY

The very configuration of Minnesota's state and local governments added to the obstacles for getting approval for a new stadium. The state's bureaucracy is not organized to promote major metropolitan projects. Metro cities and counties can do nothing without state approval, leaving big metro decisions at the mercy of politicians who have statewide constituencies: the governor and the legislature.

It's a terrible match with an ironic twist. The metro area's professional sports teams all carry the Minnesota name as if they belong to the whole state. Yet, the state shifts financial and political risk to metro governments, where destructive rivalries—especially between St. Paul and Minneapolis—produce irrational decisions. The state's insistence in the 1990s that Minneapolis and St. Paul compete for a Twins ballpark only made things worse, prolonging the agony and upping the cost.

Rejected at the capitol and distrusted for their feint to North Carolina, the Twins absorbed another blow when Minneapolis allowed the Guthrie Theater to claim the coveted riverfront site. The ball club felt more and more like a kid on the outside looking in, pressing his nose against the candy store window.

By 1999, new baseball venues had been completed in Cleveland, Denver, Dallas–Fort Worth, Atlanta, and Phoenix. Others were under construction in Milwaukee, Houston, Seattle, San Francisco, and Detroit. San Diego and Cincinnati had decided to proceed, and Pennsylvania had forged a financial package to produce ballparks in Philadelphia and Pittsburgh. Like mighty Casey, the Twins had struck out.

It was hard to imagine that all of these other cities had been wrong about baseball. No discernable wave of regret came drifting in from those places. Still, Minneapolis politicians were reluctant to embrace the Twins' stadium hopes, fearful of voter backlash. In 1997 voters had overwhelmingly passed a charter change aimed at discouraging sports stadiums in the city and limiting city spending on such projects to $10 million.

Governor Carlson recalled taking a boat tour along the historic central riverfront with Minneapolis officials on a gorgeous summer night. As they pointed out examples of redevelopment progress, Carlson waited for the magic moment when Mayor Sharon Sayles Belton would unveil her vision for a festive riverfront area, complete with ballpark, marina, and market—a place where three million visitors could come every summer to see a game while enjoying St. Anthony Falls and the historic mills. The moment never came.

Into the void stepped St. Paul Mayor Norm Coleman, fresh from his hockey triumph. Coleman had landed an NHL expansion team and, astonishingly, had coaxed the state into subsidizing an arena. In 1999, he set his sights on luring the Twins. Coleman's enthusiasm was infectious, and his talent for visualization was unmatched. In one speech he used the word "vision" 27 times. He could describe what he wanted, and he was relentless in selling his city.

The state's insistence in the 1990s that Minneapolis and St. Paul **compete** for a Twins ballpark only made things worse.

The cartoon representatives of Minneapolis and St. Paul are smiling here, but a bitter rivalry lies beneath.

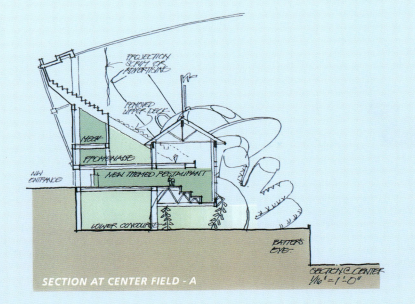

SECTION AT CENTER FIELD - A

- ■ Suites
- ■ Club Seating
- ■ Stadium Club/Restaurant
- ■ Concession
- ■ Restrooms
- ■ Retail/Office Space

Remodeling the Dome. In the late 1990s, the Metrodome's operators considered remodeling the facility exclusively for baseball. In these plans, the angle of the field was shifted slightly, and the lower deck seats were realigned. Views of the field from the main concourse were opened up. A themed restaurant with a large sculpture of a cap and glove was proposed for center field. The exterior was to be bolstered with brick and glass, but the Teflon roof stayed in place. The design didn't generate much enthusiasm from the Twins or the public.

**Metrodome Baseball Study
WEST ELEVATION**

CAPITAL CITY BALLPARK The St. Paul Option

IN 2002, THE TWINS AND THE CITY OF ST. PAUL LAUNCHED a study to analyze potential ballpark sites in or near downtown. The locations considered were: the Gateway area, opposite the Minnesota Wild's Xcel Energy Arena; the North Quadrant, on a site bordered by Jackson Street, 7th Street, and Interstate 94; Lowertown, on the Gillette Company site opposite the Farmer's Market; Lower Landing, on the riverfront spot just east of the Union Depot; and River (or West Side) Flats, across the Mississippi River from downtown. A variety of designs and layouts were considered, some incorporating retractable roofs and some involving larger neighborhood revitalization plans. The Gateway site eventually emerged as the number-one option, but a St. Paul ballpark ultimately fell through, first in a voter referendum and later when it became clear that the city lacked the infrastructure strengths that Minneapolis offered.

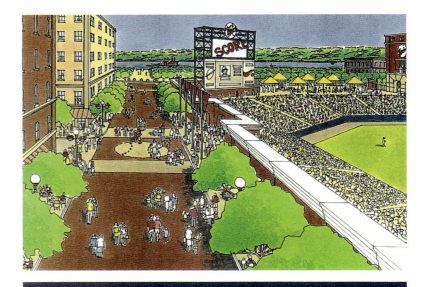

OUTDOOR BALLPARK IN SAINT PAUL

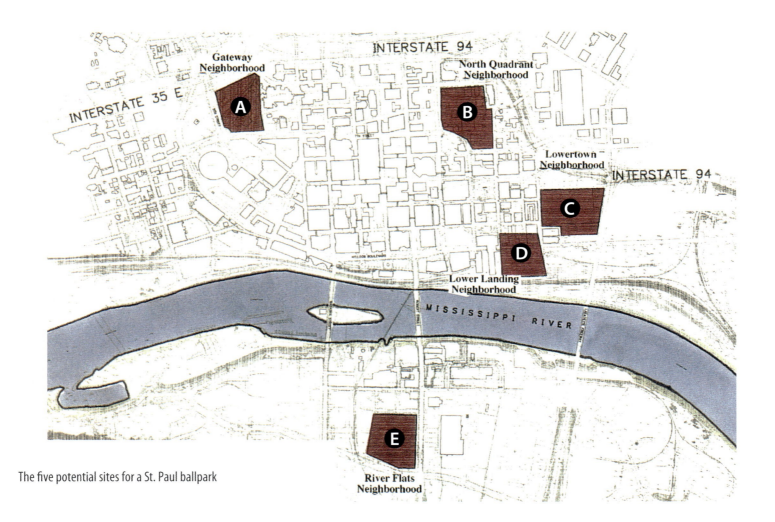

The five potential sites for a St. Paul ballpark

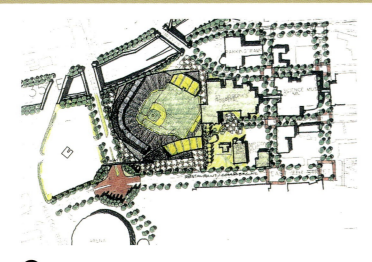

A Gateway site

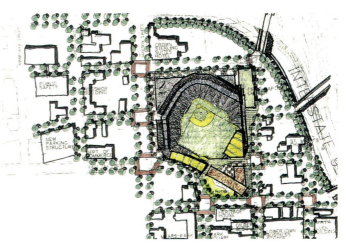

B North Quadrant site

C Lowertown site

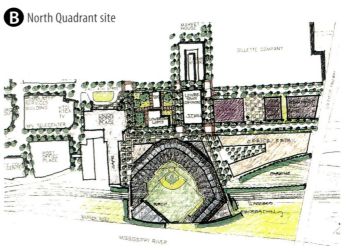

D Lower Landing site

E River Flats site

Artist's rendering of the River Flats ballpark location, with the downtown skyline in the background

BALLPARK BOOM
While Minnesota Argued, 14 Cities Built New Stadiums

Year	Market	Team	Ballpark	Capacity	Cost	Percent Gov't Funds
1992	Baltimore	Orioles	Camden Yards	48,900	$235 million	96
1994	Cleveland	Indians	Progressive Field	43,300	$173 million	87
1994	Dallas–Ft. Worth	Rangers	Rangers Ballpark	49,100	$181 million	80
1994	Twins express need for new ballpark					
1995	Denver	Rockies	Coors Field	50,500	$300 million	75
1996	Atlanta	Braves	Turner Field	50,100	$235 million	100*
1998	Phoenix	Diamondbacks	Chase Field	49,000	$355 million	76
1999	Seattle	Mariners	Safeco Field	47,100	$517 million	76
2000	Detroit	Tigers	Comerica Park	41,800	$300 million	50
2000	Houston	Astros	Minute Maid Park	41,000	$266 million	67
2000	San Francisco	Giants	AT&T Park	41,500	$319 million	5
2001	Milwaukee	Brewers	Miller Park	42,200	$322 million	64
2001	Pittsburgh	Pirates	PNC Park	38,500	$230 million	71
2003	Cincinnati	Reds	Great American Ball Park	42,100	$297 million	17
2004	Philadelphia	Phillies	Citizens Bank Park	43,600	$346 million	50
2004	San Diego	Padres	Petco Park	42,500	$411 million	70
2006	St. Louis	Cardinals	Busch Stadium	46,900	$346 million	0
2006	Minnesota passes stadium bill					
2008	Washington	Nationals	Nationals Park	41,900	$611 million	100
2009	New York	Yankees	Yankee Stadium	52,300	$1.3 billion	39
2009	New York	Mets	Citi Field	42,000	$850 million	31
2010	Minneapolis–St. Paul	Twins	Target Field	39,504	$545 million	64
2012	Miami	Marlins	Marlins Ballpark	37,000	$515 million	70

Built for 1996 Summer Olympics

Of five St. Paul ballpark sites nominated, three got most of the attention: one in Lowertown, one on the West Side flats, and the third next to the new hockey arena. St. Paul lacked the economic muscle that Minneapolis could bring to a baseball deal, however. Minneapolis' downtown workforce was three times larger. Its downtown residential population was six times larger. It had better transit service and far more hotels, restaurants, and parking spots. The heart of the Twins' fan base was in the west metro. But St. Paul had advantages aside from its excitable salesman. It had a superior natural setting and a better historic building stock. As designers liked to say, St. Paul had the bones of a great city. It also had the family attractions—the children's museum and the science museum—that Minneapolis lacked. And it had the loyalty of out-state legislators who favored St. Paul as their cozy part-time home while associating Minneapolis with crime and big-city problems.

Coleman's campaign had a chip-on-the-shoulder edge to it. St. Paul was painted as the spunky underdog. "The path to keeping the Twins in Minnesota leads to St. Paul," Bell told the mayor.

Coleman wanted St. Paul voters to approve a hike in the sales tax to pay for one-third of the $325 million venture. The team and state would split the rest. To sweeten the deal, Pohlad agreed to step down as owner, selling the team to Timberwolves owner Glen Taylor and Wild partner Bob Naegele if voters approved an open-air stadium. But they did not. The tally was lopsided. The Twins found themselves back at square one.

The cities collided again in 2002 and 2003. Coleman's successor, Randy Kelly, emphasized St. Paul's family-friendly nature. Minneapolis' new mayor, R. T. Rybak, stressed that while a ballpark wasn't his first priority, his downtown had overwhelming economic and geographic advantages. The sibling rivalry grew uglier as baseball's future in Minnesota dangled on the edge of a cliff.

CONTRACTION: FLIRTING WITH THE GUILLOTINE

Polls ran four to one against any public role in a new ballpark, no matter where it might be built. That kind of clear and persistent opposition landed the Twins—along with the Montreal Expos—on the chopping block in 2001. The comatose Expos had drawn fewer fans that season than seven minor league clubs. The Twins, although improved on the field, had made no progress toward a new stadium.

Since baseball's adoption of partial revenue sharing in the mid-1990s, financially successful teams had been subsidizing the stragglers, and some owners were growing impatient. They had given the Twins $78.6 million over six seasons, and the amounts were getting larger. More than a dozen other markets had raised $2.3 billion in public money to build new stadiums. Why should Minnesota and Montreal—the league's bottom two teams for generating stadium and other local revenue—be propped up when their cities refused to help? That was the question as negotiations began between owners and the players' union in 2001.

Whether eliminating two major league teams through contraction was a real threat or just a bargaining ploy wasn't entirely clear. Both sides had dirty hands. The players had bid up salaries, but owners had rushed in to pay them. In 2000, Alex Rodriguez signed a contract with the Texas Rangers that earned him more money in a year ($25 million) than was paid to the entire Twins roster.

"Everything is on the table, including contraction," Commissioner Bud Selig said at the 2001 World Series. The following week, the owners voted 28 to 2 to reduce the league by two teams. Selig, declining to name them, described the targeted teams as having "a long record of failing to generate enough revenues to operate a viable major league franchise." Everyone knew he meant the Expos and Twins.

In a chilling letter to Twins employees, Carl Pohlad's son Jim wrote: "Our willingness to go along with contraction, if the commissioner so decides, has come from a feeling of hopelessness. Within the context of baseball's commitment, when we are posed the question, 'Why should the Minnesota Twins not be contracted?', we are unable to find a plausible answer."

Selig blamed Minnesota's politicians and Minnesotans themselves. "There are a lot of people up there who have to look themselves in the mirror," he said.

St. Paul mayor Norm Coleman addresses reporters about the potential purchase of the Twins by Glen Taylor (middle) and Bob Naegele (right) in October 1999.

Commissioner Bud Selig, shown here in 2007, was the focus of a lot of attention in Minnesota during the contraction scare of 2002.

Commissioner Bud Selig and Governor Jesse Ventura testify before the House Judiciary Committee in December 2001 to discuss Major League Baseball's antitrust exemption and the question of contraction.

A LOW POINT GETS LOWER

For Twins fans, the ballpark saga had reached its lowest point. The day they most feared had arrived. Carl Pohlad would get to choose: Did he want to *write* a big check to build a ballpark by himself? Or, did he want to *receive* a big check from the league for folding the team? From what the public saw, Pohlad seemed happy to take the check. A mercy killing was at hand.

The air was thick with recriminations aimed at Major League Baseball for its willful greed, at Pohlad for his string of mistakes, at Minnesotans for their self-righteousness. The gloom and the paranoia were palpable. Why us? Were the Florida teams being saved because of the state's connections to the Bush family? Were the Twins being sacrificed to enhance Selig's hometown Milwaukee Brewers? Conspiracy theories aside, the Twin Cities had had a gun to its head from the day Camden Yards opened in 1992. Other cities had taken out insurance policies in the form of new ballparks. Minnesota had thumbed its collective nose. Now came the consequence.

Hennepin County District Court Judge Harry Crump

But the scare lasted only 91 days. The Twins' Metrodome landlords took the matter immediately to court, where Hennepin County District Court Judge Harry Crump struck the big blow against contraction. His ruling, upheld by the Court of Appeals, became affectionately known as "Homer Hankie Jurisprudence." Crump pointed out that baseball's legal history makes the game more than an ordinary private enterprise. The Twins cannot be separated from the fabric of the community, he said, citing the team's world championships and its list of baseball legends. "Clearly more than money is at stake," the judge said. "The vital public interest, or trust, of the Twins substantially outweighs any private interest."

Crump was throwing baseball's prized anti-trust exemption back in its face. If Major League Baseball wanted to maintain its privileged status as a public trust, then it could not act as an ordinary business. It could not simply lop off weaker teams to fatten its bottom line.

"Despite what he said, I don't believe that Carl would ever have agreed to contraction," Bell later noted. "Why not? Family pressure." Pohlad cared a lot about his family and its reputation, Bell said. He didn't want his name to be ranked with the O'Malleys, Irsays, and Modells—families that had notoriously moved teams and betrayed hometowns.

"Baseball crosses social barriers, creates **community spirit**,

and is much more than a private enterprise."

—*Harry Crump, Hennepin County District Court Judge*

As momentum gained for a Warehouse District location for the new ballpark, this rendering depicted it in its setting—offering an almost Gothic feel to the nighttime scene.

REVIVAL ON THE FIELD—AND AT THE DRAWING BOARD

Maybe, as Samuel Johnson suggested, nothing concentrates the mind like the prospect of a hanging. The threat of contraction coincided with a remarkable turnaround on the field for the Twins and a thaw in the stadium freeze.

In an attempt to re-energize the team, Jim Pohlad suggested a youth movement: Let the kids play and see what happens. What happened was amazing. Baseball in the Twin Cities took a big turn for the better in 2001. The Twins ended their horrid stretch of eight straight losing seasons by leading the division for much of the summer before finishing in second place with an 85–77 record. Doug Mientkiewicz, Corey Koskie, and A. J. Pierzynski had breakout years. Torii Hunter emerged as a rising star. Joe Mays, Eric Milton, and Brad Radke formed a solid core on the mound. A new marketing campaign, "Get to know 'em," was a hit. Attendance jumped 80 percent, and TV ratings soared. There was life in the corpse after all.

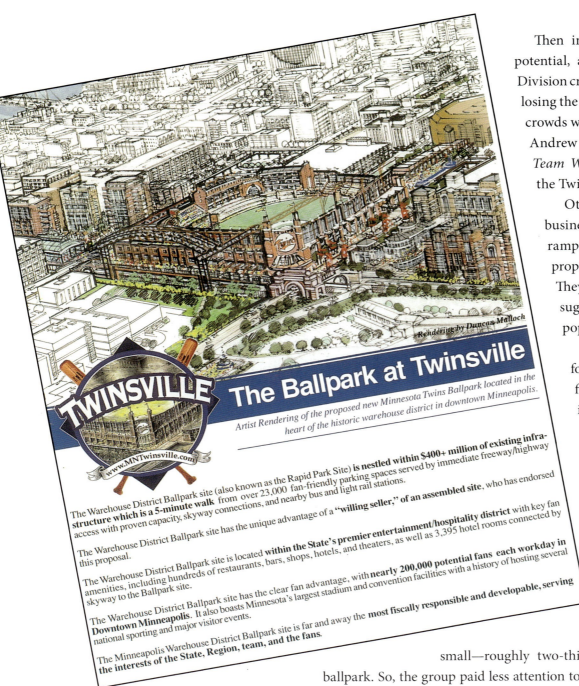

The Ballpark at Twinsville

Artist Rendering of the proposed new Minnesota Twins Ballpark located in the heart of the historic warehouse district in downtown Minneapolis.

TWINSVILLE
www.MNTwinsville.com

Rendering by Duncan Malloch

The Warehouse District Ballpark site (also known as the Rapid Park Site) **is nestled within $400+ million of existing infrastructure which is a 5-minute walk** from over 23,000 fan-friendly parking spaces served by immediate freeway/highway access with proven capacity, skyway connections, and nearby bus and light rail stations.

The Warehouse District Ballpark site has the unique advantage of a **"willing seller,"** of an assembled site, who has endorsed this proposal.

The Warehouse District Ballpark site is located **within the State's premier entertainment/hospitality district** with key fan amenities, including hundreds of restaurants, bars, shops, hotels, and theaters, as well as 3,395 hotel rooms connected by skyway to the Ballpark site.

The Warehouse District Ballpark site has the clear fan advantage, with **nearly 200,000 potential fans each workday in Downtown Minneapolis**. It also boasts Minnesota's largest stadium and convention facilities with a history of hosting several national sporting and major visitor events.

The Minneapolis Warehouse District Ballpark site is far and away the **most fiscally responsible and developable, serving the interests of the State, Region, team, and the fans**.

This brochure was released touting the advantages of a Twins ballpark in the Warehouse District, on the site of the Rapid Park parking lot behind Target Center.

Then in 2002, Johan Santana previewed his star potential, and the Twins ran away with the Central Division crown. They beat Oakland in the playoffs before losing the American League pennant to the Angels. The crowds were back, and roaring. As baseball economist Andrew Zimbalist observed in his book *May the Best Team Win*, "Divine justice seemed to intervene for the Twins."

Other things were happening, too. Minneapolis businessmen Bruce Lambrecht and Rich Pogin ramped up their campaign for a ballpark on property they owned in the Warehouse District. They called their concept "Twinsville" as a way to suggest that Minneapolis could imitate Chicago's popular Wrigleyville neighborhood.

Meanwhile, civic and business leaders formed New Ballpark Inc. to explore a privately financed solution. The initiative was unusual in a number of ways: It sought advice from opponents, including State Senator John Marty; it showed extreme interest in how a ballpark would fit into the surrounding neighborhood; and it recognized that the Lambrecht-Pogin property was a potential transportation crossroads, with freeways, transit lines, and bike trails converging and an ample supply of parking already available. These would all become important points.

The biggest problem was that the site was small—roughly two-thirds the size required for a new-generation ballpark. So, the group paid less attention to new stadiums as models than they did to old ones, particularly Chicago's classic bandbox, Wrigley Field, built in 1914.

The group considered the community to be its chief client, not the Twins. If a ballpark were to be built, it would be on the community's terms. Its primary purpose would be as a gathering place, rather than a vessel to improve the team's bottom line. The Twins and Major League Baseball could take it or leave it. At least, that was the group's initial stance.

As momentum returned for a downtown ballpark in Minneapolis in the early 2000s, five sites emerged as the top contenders, including Target Field's eventual site in the Warehouse District (site 1) as well as the current site of the Metrodome.

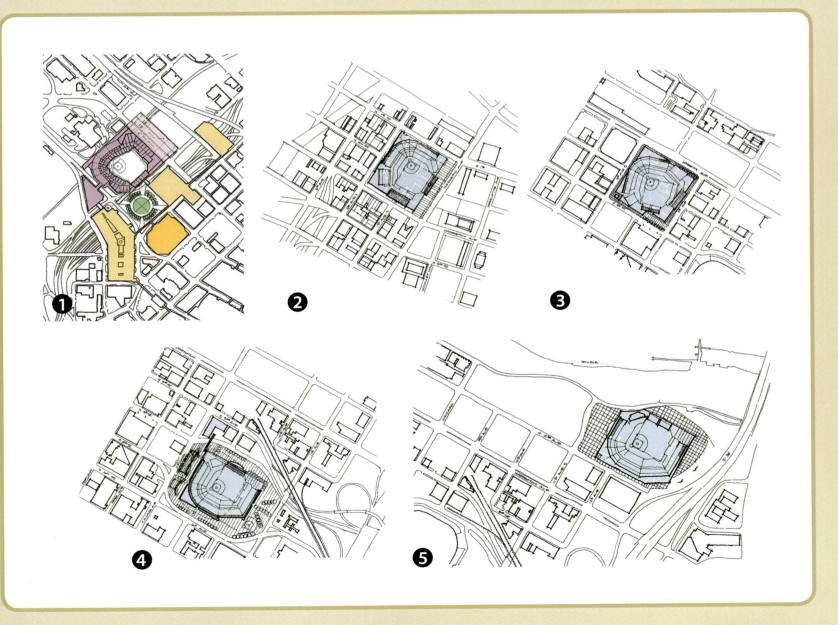

Hennepin County Commissioner Mike Opat (right)
with Minneapolis Mayor R. T. Rybak, April 2002

NOW BATTING: HENNEPIN COUNTY

When private financing proved unrealistic, New Ballpark Inc. turned to Hennepin County as its government partner. Baseball was just one area into which the county had begun to assert a leadership role on metro issues. On transit, health care, libraries, parks, and street design, the Hennepin County Board, influenced mainly by Mike Opat and Peter McLaughlin, was wading into territory that the city, state, and Metropolitan Council could not seem to handle. As Opat put it, somebody had to step up to the big city challenges. Opat's role, and the county's role over the next several years, would be paramount in solving the baseball dilemma.

After yet another study commission's report, the legislature opened a round of hearings in 2002 with St. Paul and Minneapolis still in a dogfight and Opat serving as Minneapolis' point man. But his testimony got a cool reception from Representative Ron Abrams of Minnetonka, the House tax chairman. Abrams disliked the idea of the state's largest local government getting into the stadium game. In the end, the 2002 legislature did pass a stadium bill, but one that excluded Hennepin County. St. Paul was the only option for a ballpark. A joyous party erupted outside the House chamber among the St. Paul contingent.

But the joy was short-lived. A *Star Tribune* editorial immediately exposed the flaw in the legislation. By cutting out Hennepin County, the legislature had failed to leverage more than a half billion dollars of government investments already made in freeways, transit, and parking ramps adjacent to the Minneapolis site. In so doing, lawmakers had tossed aside the very characteristic—urban critical mass—that makes the modern ballpark successful.

Indeed, when the Twins sat down to negotiate with St. Paul officials, they quickly discovered that the proposed site, across from the Xcel Energy arena, would require additional infrastructure (mostly freeway ramps) costing $50 million. It was clear that the legislature had passed a bill that couldn't produce a ballpark. "When we considered the lower revenue in St. Paul, the parking problems, and then discovered the infrastructure costs, it just didn't work," Bell said.

The old real estate maxim was slowly sinking in: location, location, location. The built-in advantages of the Minneapolis site were too hard to ignore.

IT TAKES A GOVERNOR

In most major league markets, mayors drive the important public projects. In the Twin Cities market, however, governors set the tone for all big decisions. The Twins' ballpark odyssey tested the patience of three governors.

Arne Carlson was frustrated with growing commercialism in sports and the lack of civic responsibility among athletes and owners. Yet, from his boyhood in the Bronx he understood what it meant to lose a baseball team. His beloved New York Giants had joined the Brooklyn Dodgers in pulling up stakes in 1958 and moving to California.

"It devastated the community," he said, and that's why he tried, albeit unsuccessfully, to help the Twins.

Jesse Ventura, governor from 1999 to 2003, was less interested in a solution than in ranting against public financing, even though he had made his own fortune as a professional wrestler in arenas built with big chunks of public money.

Tim Pawlenty, as a conservative leader in the legislature, had never supported the Twins' stadium drive. Yet, as governor, he felt a wider responsibility and ultimately crafted a solution that perfectly matched his governing style: shift the financial burden and political risk to local government and then, if it works, claim credit.

By 2004, it was clear that the burden and risk had shifted fully to Hennepin County. Hennepin was the only local government big enough to play the stadium game. The costs, after all, had more than doubled during Minnesota's decade of indecision while the options narrowed. The prime riverfront land that the Twins coveted had been lost. And a retractable roof, once a necessity, had become an unaffordable frill.

The Twins were entering their ninth year as a supplicant. Hundreds of hours of hearings, thousands of pages of testimony, stacks of stadium renderings, scores of studies, and seven blue ribbon panels had failed to resolve the issue. Pawlenty's appointing of another task force was no surprise; the surprise was his reframing of the issue. No longer was the question *whether* to build a ballpark, but *when and where?* "Bottom line," he declared. "I don't want to lose the Twins or the Vikings on my watch."

Minneapolis' economic development director Lee Sheehy sensed a now-or-never moment. In November 2003, he convinced Mayor Rybak and the city council to set aside their emotions on the political aspects to consider solely the economic question: If there were to be a ballpark, what location would make the most sense? His report to the governor's task force, issued jointly with Hennepin County, made an overwhelming case for the Warehouse District site. The site took advantage of huge investments already made in parking, transit, and freeways, and it was owned by a single, willing seller. "It's far and away the most fiscally responsible site," he concluded.

THE TWINS–HENNEPIN COUNTY PARTNERSHIP

The legislature ignored Sheehy's report in 2004, but it could not ignore what happened in the spring of 2005. April 26 would go down as a historic day. The Twins and Hennepin County announced a financial partnership to build a ballpark in the Warehouse District, on the Rapid Park parking lot site. The Twins would pay one-third of the projected cost up front. The county would raise the rest by hiking the sales tax by 15 hundredths of a penny. The increase would amount to 3 cents on a $20 purchase, excluding groceries, clothing, and medicine. A week later, on May 3, four of the seven commissioners—Opat, McLaughlin, Mark Stenglein, and Randy Johnson—swallowed hard and voted to pursue the project. Each knew that his political career might be over.

The Warehouse District, or Rapid Park, site took advantage of the area's existing infrastructure while allowing for the possibility for further growth and development.

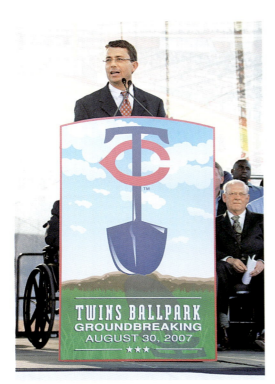

Mike Opat at the ballpark groundbreaking, August 2007

"It just seemed to me that it fell to us to do it," Opat said. "I thought the Twins might leave in the long term. It wasn't a perfect solution. But I don't think we live in the world of the ideal; we live in the world of the possible. I asked myself if we were going to be better off with the Twins or without them. I thought we'd be better off with them. That was my thinking."

Opat said all four commissioners endured threats, abusive phone calls, and picketers in front of their homes. "It's tough when the kids are crying because they don't know what's happening, or like when I've got my daughter in my arms after church and a woman is berating me." It was especially hard, he said, to get private encouragement from politicians who didn't dare favor the project in public.

The four commissioners had taken Pawlenty's bait and left the state off the hook. All the legislature needed to do was bless the deal and step aside. But that's not what happened, at least not right away.

Lawmakers fell to bickering about whether they should order the county to impose a referendum. Polls showed clearly that voters wanted a direct say. State law allowed referendums in such cases, but it also allowed exemptions. In practice, elected officials routinely decided all kinds of unpopular tax issues without direct votes of the people. The Twins and the county board majority were clear on this point: If the legislature imposed a referendum, they would scuttle their deal. Legislators responded by failing to act. The ballpark was stalled again.

THE MINNESOTA BALLPARK AUTHORITY

Who Owns Target Field?

In approving the joint venture of Hennepin County and the Twins to build Target Field, the Minnesota State Legislature created a public body, the Minnesota Ballpark Authority, to oversee construction and operations. The MBA owns the site and the ballpark on behalf of the public, and it leases the ballpark to the Twins, who are responsible for operating and caring for the property. The lease expires in 2040, with two 10-year renewal options. The ball club's yearly rent starts at $900,000, with an escalator for inflation. That money is placed in a fund to finance future renovations.

The team, meanwhile, is allowed to retain all revenues from selling tickets, club seats, suites, and corporate sponsorships, including naming rights.

The state gets the first right to buy the team if it is put up for sale. If the team is sold, the Minnesota Ballpark Authority gets a portion of the windfall. If the team is dissolved or relocated, the state gets all rights to the Twins name, logos, colors, and heritage.

A five-member board governs the MBA. The governor and Hennepin County each appoint two members, and the City of Minneapolis appoints one. The board hires and employs an executive director and staff.

OCTOBER SURPRISE

Opat and Bell had given up. An election year in 2006 made it suicidal to revive the ballpark project. But Pawlenty surprised everyone by calling the parties to the governor's mansion on a Sunday night in October 2005. He asked them to try again. Bell declined. The Twins wouldn't go forward without assurances that all four caucus leaders—Matt Entenza and Steve Sviggum in the House and Dean Johnson and Dick Day in the Senate—would guarantee a once-and-for-all, up-or-down vote on the stalled 2005 bill, without the referendum requirement. All four agreed.

"The atmosphere was much more supportive," Sviggum recalled. "We could go around the state—everywhere but Hennepin County—and tell people that a new ballpark wasn't going to cost them a dime." A solution was very near.

The bill passed on May 21, 2006, by ten votes in the House and two in the Senate. The ordeal was suddenly over. After a decade of delay and recriminations, Minnesota would get its ballpark. Bell, who had prowled the halls of the Capitol for ten years, was exhausted and ecstatic. "It was the hardest thing I had ever done," he said. "I knew that we finally had it."

In ideological terms, the victory was extraordinary. Stadium supporters had found enough pragmatists from each party to break an uncommonly solid coalition of liberals and conservatives that had stopped the project at every turn by invoking the most potent force in Minnesota politics and culture: populist anger against perceived elitism. Rather than help pay for a ballpark, Minnesotans would be better off without the Twins—or so the argument went. Eventually it ran out of steam.

"In the end, they just wore us down," noted longtime ballpark opponent John Marty. "They tried a thousand things and finally found something that worked." He referred to the final deal that took state legislators off the hook, leaving the Hennepin County commissioners to take the heat. But there wasn't much heat. In November, all four commissioners were re-elected by comfortable margins. In fact, no elected official in the decade-long battle lost an election because of the stadium issue.

It took a bipartisan effort with no state money, no retractable roof, a specific site, a broad, moderate local tax increase, a measure of courage, and loads of patience. "Everybody learned along the way," said Bob Starkey, the Twins' financial consultant.

Jerry Bell, president of Twins Sports Inc., during the final hours of the Minnesota House debate on the stadium bill, April 26, 2006.

Dave St. Peter, president of the Minnesota Twins, gives the thumbs up after the House passed the stadium bill on May 20, 2006.

With Carl Pohlad at his side, Governor Tim Pawlenty signs into the law the Twins stadium bill on May 26, 2006.

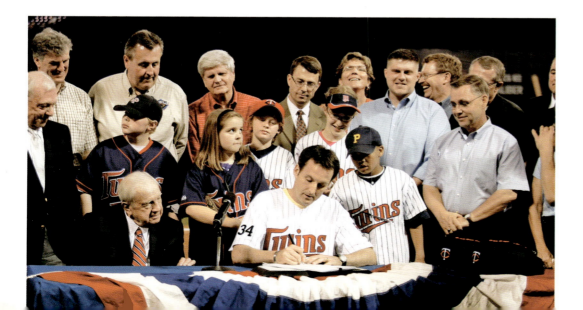

Groundbreaking ceremony for the new ballpark, August 30, 2007

A $29 million parking lot

A FINAL SNAG

Opat was elated over the bill's passage, but his problems weren't over. Legislators had set an extraordinarily tight limit on the public cost of land and surrounding infrastructure ($90 million). Money needed for attractive walkways, bridges, transit stations, and connections to downtown would be sufficient only if the land price remained reasonable. The county, two years earlier, had signed an option (since expired) to buy the land from Lambrecht and Pogin for $12 million. But the landowners were miffed when the county insisted that some of their property go to the Twins for VIP parking, and they were upset about being excluded from legislative negotiations. They waited in the summer of 2006 for Opat to make a new offer on the land. No offer came. The county assumed the old price was still in play, but Lambrecht and Pogin wanted more money.

The dispute landed in condemnation court, with Opat offering $8 million and the landowners holding out for $65 million—75 percent of the county's infrastructure limit. Tempers rose before a $29 million settlement was finally reached. The Twins helped fill the infrastructure shortfall by spending an additional $24 million on public spaces.

It took a bipartisan effort

with no state money,

no retractable roof,

a specific site, a broad,

moderate local tax increase,

a measure of courage—and

loads of **patience**.

CHECK, PLEASE?
Adding up Target Field's Costs

New ballpark costs	**$440 million**
Paid by Twins	$180 million
Paid by Hennepin County	$260 million
Infrastructure costs	**$105 million**
Paid by Twins	$15 million
Paid by Hennepin County	$90 million
Total costs	**$545 million**
Paid by Twins	$195 million (36 percent)
Paid by Hennepin County	$350 million (64 percent)

The Twins approved increases of $45.5 million beyond the original $130 million budget for fan amenities and ballpark enhancements. In addition, the Twins provided $4.5 million in funding for Target Plaza, which was matched by Target Corporation. The team also contributed $15 million for infrastructure costs, above and beyond the original budget.

Carl Pohlad making his final visit to the ballpark construction site, June 20, 2008

"I can't believe it,

I just can't **believe** it,"

Pohlad told Bell at the sight

of the massive project.

CROSSING HOME PLATE

Construction on the new ballpark began on May 21, 2007, nearly 13 years after Carl Pohlad first expressed his desire for a new home for the Twins. The structure itself would cost $440 million, about 60 percent from the public and 40 percent from the ball club. Land and public infrastructure would cost an additional $105 million, 86 percent from the public and 14 percent from the Twins and Target Corporation.

Pohlad, propped in a wheelchair, visited the construction site for the last time on June 20, 2008. "I can't believe it, I just can't believe it," he told Bell at the sight of the massive project.

Carl Pohlad died on January 5, 2009. He was 93. More than 1,400 mourners packed the Basilica of St. Mary in downtown Minneapolis for his funeral mass, showing, perhaps, the willingness of Minnesotans to see a man's life and work—and the generous gifts of his family—in wider perspective. Carl Pohlad was no longer the villain.

"When we bought the Twins, we had no concept of what it would mean to own a baseball team, the emotional involvement of the public that went with it," Jim Pohlad recalled later. "And we had no concept of the process of what it would take to build a new stadium. We were naïve about all of that."

The depth of the emotion that came with owning the Twins and building a ballpark was a "double-edged sword for the family," he said. "It was a huge learning process." Baseball, as it turned out, was not just another business.

THE LONG TRIP TO TARGET FIELD *A Timeline*

1994	Twins owner Carl Pohlad tells the Metropolitan Sports Facilities Commission that the team needs a new ballpark because the Metrodome doesn't deliver enough revenue to allow the team to compete with other clubs.
1996	The Minnesota State Legislature rejects a proposal for a state referendum on a new Twins ballpark.
1997	The legislature rejects a plan to build a retractable-roof ballpark along the river in downtown Minneapolis. The plan included a state loan to Pohlad in exchange for the state getting part ownership in the team.
1998	Pohlad agrees to sell the Twins to North Carolina businessman Don Beaver if voters in Greensboro agree to build a ballpark; the referendum fails.
1999	The Twins turn to St. Paul, but city voters defeat a stadium plan and legislators reject public ownership of the team.
2000	New Ballpark Inc., a group of Minneapolis business and civic leaders, explores a privately financed ballpark solution. The Twins launch a citizens committee aimed at keeping the franchise alive.
2001	Major League Baseball owners vote to eliminate two teams, believed to be the Twins and the Montreal Expos.
2002	Hennepin County District Court Judge Harry Crump blocks contraction of the Twins. Legislature passes a St. Paul–only ballpark bill, but negotiations fail to produce a stadium.
2003	Governor Tim Pawlenty launches a screening committee to examine baseball and football sites in the Twin Cities.
2004	The governor's committee recommends action, but the legislature rejects all plans.
2005	The Twins and Hennepin County form a partnership to build a ballpark in the Warehouse District of Minneapolis; the legislature rejects the plan because it lacks a referendum.
2006	The Minnesota State Legislature approves the Hennepin-Twins plan, and the Hennepin County Board passes a sales tax increase to help finance the ballpark.
2007	Construction on the new ballpark begins.
2008	A dispute over the land's selling price between Hennepin County and property owners is resolved in court. The Twins announce a 25-year naming-rights agreement with Target Corporation. The ballpark is named Target Field.
2009	The scoreboard, grass, and seats are installed as the ballpark nears completion.
2010	The Twins play the Boston Red Sox in Target Field's first regular-season game.

An early artist's rendering of a ballpark on the Rapid Park site in the Warehouse District

3

LINES ON PAPER

A Ballpark Takes Shape

"The new ballpark for Minnesota

will be a **defining testament**

to a team, a state, and its people."

—*Earl Santee, principal architect, Populous*

Baseball, more than other sports, is emotionally connected to its architecture. The game has a strong sense of place. It's hard to imagine the Cubs without Wrigley Field or the Red Sox without Fenway Park. One day, perhaps, it will be impossible to imagine the Twins without Target Field. A good ballpark is more than just a home, it's part of a team's DNA.

The idiosyncrasies of the game itself exaggerate the role of architecture, and vice versa. The possibility of varied field dimensions—like the close left-field wall in Boston or the large foul territory in Oakland—allows a ballpark to change the way the game is played from one city to the next. Baseball's deliberate pace also allows fans the time to look around between pitches and to wander through the stands during the middle innings. Baseball, in that way, is less a sport than a sensual pastime, less a sharp focus than a wide-angle experience that invites its followers to absorb and savor their surroundings.

Baseball buildings over the years have assumed an architectural category all their own. Devotees know the special traits of each place—the ivy-covered walls of Chicago's Wrigley Field, the Green Monster in Boston, McCovey Cove in San Francisco, the Clemente Bridge in Pittsburgh, the upper-deck frieze in the Bronx, the B&O Warehouse building in Baltimore. Architecture becomes part of the fan experience, and fans of the game come to know a great ballpark when they experience one.

From the start of the Target Field project, the Twins and the community pushed the designers to deliver more than just a ballpark; they wanted a piece of civic architecture, one that would overcome a difficult site and connect intimately to its surroundings.

To take on the challenge, the Twins turned to Populous (formerly known as HOK Sport), the world's leading designer of sports venues. The firm, headquartered in Kansas City, designed 16 of the 21 major league ballparks built in the period from 1992 to 2012, as well as more than 60 minor league and spring training facilities. Earl Santee, the principal architect on the Minneapolis job, had left his imprint on many of those projects, particularly the new big league facilities in Denver, Pittsburgh, Houston, St. Louis, and Washington. He also led the design team on the lavish new Yankee Stadium in New York, opened in 2009.

The Minnesota job provided new and, in some ways, extreme challenges for Santee and his team. The ballpark's location, its snug fit and integration into the fabric of downtown Minneapolis, made for an extraordinary project, and the difficulties provided extra motivation for both clients and architects. "Nothing was easy about the site," Santee said. "It was the hardest site we had ever worked with."

"We wanted a piece of architecture that wasn't a monument but was part of the **community**."

—*Jim Pohlad, owner and CEO, Minnesota Twins*

Before (above) and after (below).

POPULOUS An All-Star in Sports Architecture

Earl Santee, Populous

POPULOUS, FORMERLY HOK SPORT VENUE EVENT, is among the most prolific and influential designers of sports stadiums in the world. The company's portfolio of nearly a thousand projects includes the new Wembley, Emirates, and Wimbledon Centre Court stadiums in London and the Nanjing Sports Park in Jiangsu Province, China.

The company has led architectural teams on scores of top U.S. gathering places, among them the NFL stadiums in Phoenix and Houston, college stadiums at the universities of Washington and Minnesota, and 16 of the 21 new-generation ballparks, including new homes for the Yankees, Mets, and Cardinals.

Some critics decry the firm's baseball designs as formulaic and nostalgic. But its groundbreaking Camden Yards project in 1992 reinvented the modern ballpark in ways that preserved baseball's classic elements while producing revenues that the modern game requires. Populous pushed its Baltimore innovations further in Denver (1994), San Francisco (2000), and San Diego (2004) by connecting ballparks more intimately to cities. The ultimate expression of that comes with Target Field, where a stylish piece of contemporary architecture fits into an extremely compact urban setting in a way that merges ballpark and surroundings.

Creating structures that transform neighborhoods, revive cities, and connect people are among the company's goals. In a fragmented world it's imperative that surroundings affect lives in positive ways, company executives say.

Founded in 1983, HOK was the first all-sports architecture firm. Despite consistent public opposition to spending public money on professional sports, the firm has grown steadily, along with the idea that well-designed sports venues can produce not only money for teams but social and economic benefits for cities. Populous, headquartered in Kansas City, has 10 offices worldwide.

Chicago's Wrigley Field, built in 1914, is a consensus favorite among baseball enthusiasts and purists. Along with Boston's eccentric Fenway Park (1912), Wrigley is one of only two classic ballparks remaining. The graceful interior lines, ivy-covered walls, manually operated scoreboard, and intimate relationship with its surroundings make Wrigley an architectural gem appreciated beyond the baseball world. A visit to Wrigley for an afternoon game is a must for any fan.

Dodger Stadium in Los Angeles, opened in 1962, is considered the best example from the mid-century period. Its pastel colors, wavy outfield canopies, and sunny, panoramic views epitomize the southern California experience and are enough to make Beach Boys music start running in your head. A relatively new facility in relation to the age of the sport, Dodger Stadium stands as the third oldest active ballpark in the majors, after Fenway and Wrigley.

Baltimore's Camden Yards, completed in 1992, was the first—and many argue is still the best—of the postmodern ballparks that recaptured the essence of baseball's golden age, and it inspired a whole new approach to stadiums. By using red brick and exposed steel beams while also incorporating modern amenities, Camden Yards has the flavor of both old and new. Camden's retro charm has been copied so many times in so many cities, however, that it has become almost ordinary.

"Target Field is the most **urban** ballpark we've done. It's the modern-day Wrigley Field."

—*Earl Santee, architect, Populous*

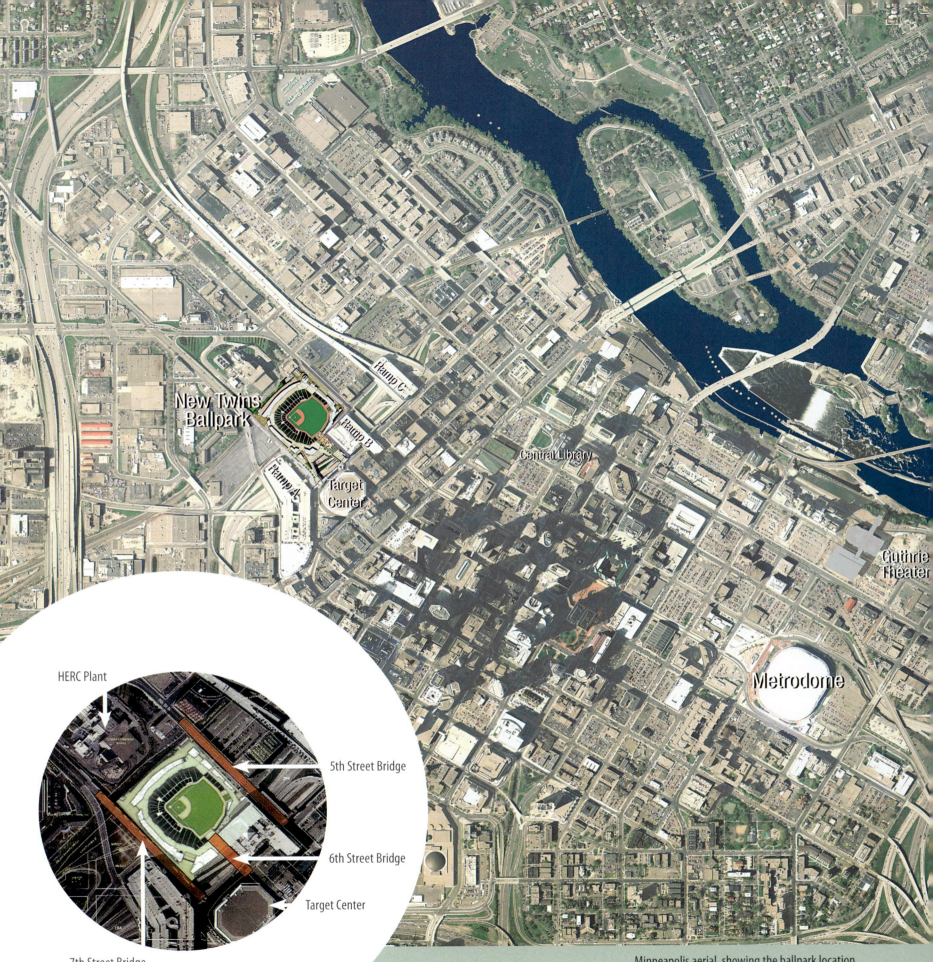

New Twins
Ballpark

Ramp C

Ramp B

Ramp A

Target
Center

Central Library

Guthrie
Theater

Metrodome

HERC Plant

5th Street Bridge

6th Street Bridge

Target Center

7th Street Bridge

Minneapolis aerial, showing the ballpark location

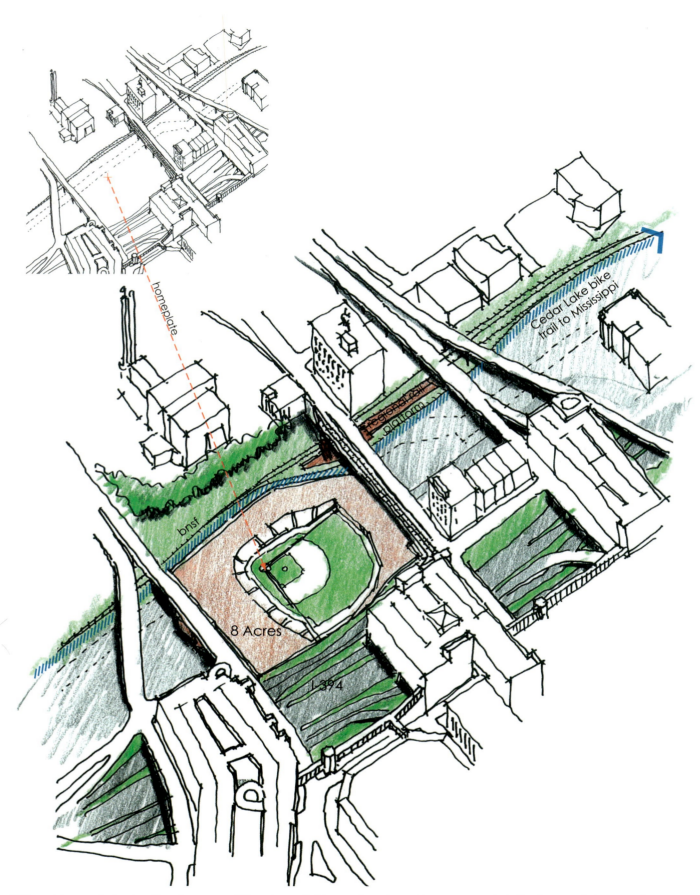

With an eight-acre site bordered by a freeway, a rail line, elevated bridges, and massive parking structures, the ballpark site made for a snug fit.

MORE THAN A BALLPARK Target Field and Its Neighborhood

THE TYPICAL STADIUM IS LIKE YOUR FAVORITE CHAIR. Pick it up and move it to another room, and it works just fine. Target Field isn't like that. It's more like a window seat fastened to its surroundings, customized to fit.

To be sure, if the Twins' new ballpark were to stand alone, it would make a beautiful building. But it's designed specifically *not* to stand alone—and that makes it all the more beautiful, and valuable, to the community.

It's more than a ballpark.

Target Field is a gathering place. It's a bridge between neighborhoods, a catalyst for redevelopment, and a harbinger of new lifestyles and habits.

Rather than turning its back to its surroundings, Target Field beckons visitors with glassy outcroppings that reach to the city. From within its walls, a giant "picture window" shows off the skyline beyond the right-field fence, then morphs into a handsome plaza, which then becomes a series of walkways flowing toward the center of downtown. The left-field corner doubles as a rail station, and a bike trail running beneath the third-base stands offers another lifeline between ballpark and community. And local streets, many of them with new paving, lighting, and trees, invite visitors to enjoy not just a ballgame but the experience of being near Target Field.

Being "more than a ballpark" defined the project from the start. Public partners wanted to make sure that Hennepin County's tax dollars generated benefits beyond baseball. The Twins, trapped for three decades in the suffocating Metrodome, wanted a home that embraced its surroundings and inspired affection in return. And they wanted a home that would lean forward, into the future.

"You can see it in the design," said Bill Blanski, an architect from the Minneapolis firm HGA, a partner in the project. "It's got a lean to it. Its geometry and form appear to be in motion. It reaches out to grab the space of the city, but the neighborhood is also invited back in."

New urban ballparks like Target Field invite people to relearn the joys of city life that decades of suburban life have conditioned many to forget. For urban life—and urban baseball—it's not just about the destination; the journey is part of the experience. With Target Field, you're more likely to walk to the ballpark, noticing things and people you wouldn't notice in your car. If you decide to take a bus or train, you might encounter an old friend also bound for the game, or you might strike up a conversation with a complete stranger wearing the jersey of your favorite player. After the game, rather than rush to the car to beat the traffic, you're more inclined to amble to a nearby pub to discuss the finer points of the game you've just seen.

Target Field invites fans to partake in a wider experience beyond the game itself—and that's something new for Twins fans.

Baseball's value to a community cannot be easily measured. There aren't enough blades of grass in Target Field's outfield to count the ways that the Twins have affected the lives of people in the Upper Midwest over the last half-century. The crack of the bat, the pop of the mitt, and now, with outdoor baseball, the warmth of the summer sun on the back of the neck bring a value to life that economists cannot calculate. Twins followers, given their team's near-death experience in 2002, take special delight in a new ballpark. They are the secular recipients of an amazing grace. Their team was lost, and now it is found.

The Twins' new home was designed to be integral to its surroundings, and some early plans included the ballpark as part of a larger neighborhood revitalization program, complete with residential construction and green spaces.

EXISTING BUILDING

NEW BUILDING

BALLPARK

DEVELOPMENT RECAP

15 STORY BUILDINGS (4)	555 UNITS
10 STORY BUILDINGS (9)	1476 UNITS
3 STORY TOWNHOMES	36 UNITS
TOTAL UNITS	2087 UNITS
UNDERGROUND PARKING	2000 SPACES
SURFACE PARKING	90 SPACES

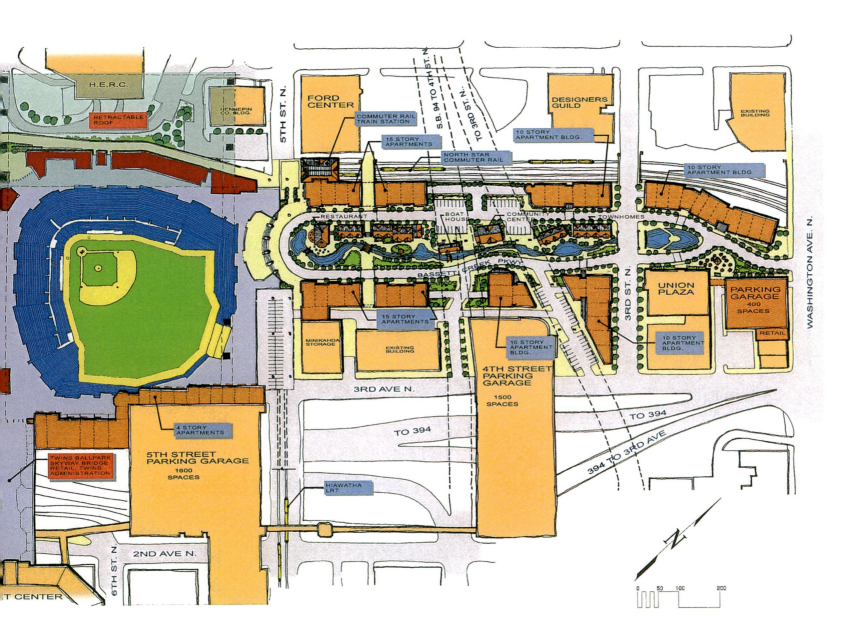

"Baseball gives us a chance to **reintroduce** ourselves.

We need to let people from greater Minnesota know that they can be comfortable here

in the city, that we like them and are happy to have them visit us."

—Mike Christenson, director of community planning and economic development, City of Minneapolis

THE WAREHOUSE DISTRICT

A HUNDRED YEARS BEFORE "TWINS TERRITORY," THE WAREHOUSE DISTRICT HAD A BUSINESS TERRITORY that covered similar ground. Beginning in the 1860s, wholesalers shipped vast numbers of agricultural implements to rapidly mechanizing farms and ranches from Wisconsin and Iowa to eastern Montana. By the early 1900s, loading farm machinery onto trains had become a way of life in the district. By the 1920s, the business had eclipsed flour milling as Minneapolis' foremost enterprise and made the city one of the world's top distribution points for agricultural supplies.

The business required rail yards, broad streets, big loading docks, and buildings with sizable shoulders. A handsome stock of 6- to 12-story brick fortresses rose to dominate the area. Eventually, the district was listed on the National Register of Historic Places and protected by city and state preservation agencies.

Baseball also claims a piece of Warehouse District lore. From 1889 to 1896, the Minneapolis Millers played in a tiny wooden bandbox called Athletic Park on First Avenue, a spot later occupied by Butler Square. Across Second Avenue, a railroad yard filled the space where Target Field now stands.

The area fell to neglect during the Great Depression of the 1930s. Artists, seeing potential in the abandoned buildings, attempted a revival in the 1970s, but higher rents chased them out after Target Center opened in 1989. Restaurants, nightclubs, and residential lofts trickled in. The sequence was similar in dozens of U.S. cities with decaying industrial districts, although Minneapolis' transition from "crumbling to cool" has been more cautious than most.

Most locals consider the Warehouse District larger than its official footprint. In everyday parlance, it covers a broad, 120-block stretch from the leafy riverfront almost to the Basilica of St. Mary, near Loring Park. It includes Target Center, the Farmers' Market, International Market Square, the Federal Reserve Bank, the North Loop neighborhood, and a crisscross of freeways and railroads. It has two main thoroughfares: First Avenue, a spine of popular nightclubs and music cafes; and Washington Avenue, a wide street meant mostly for trucks but now lined with lofts and eccentric shops. Advertising and architecture firms, web designers, and other creative businesses occupy the upper floors of these turn-of-the-century buildings. Down below, stylish young singles, some with colorful hair, pierced body parts, and tattoos, inhabit the sidewalks.

Close to the river, the district has transformed into charming loft conversions and coffee shops. But the blocks closer to Target Field are still on the urban frontier. Historic buildings are interspersed with sparse parking lots, creating perhaps a hundred opportunities for new offices, shops, and condos.

"Livability" has become a persistent theme as residents push for tree-lined sidewalks, better lighting, and more retail opportunities. Where once there was nothing but broken windows and broken pavement, young singles, empty nesters, and new parents pushing baby carriages have begun to appear. For 400 years America has been characterized by the breaking of new ground. Now the challenge is to remake old ground for new purposes. The arrival of Target Field may quicken the pace for Minneapolis' Warehouse District.

More than a century before the opening of Target Field, another baseball field, Athletic Park, was located in Minneapolis' Warehouse District.

NO PLACE FOR A BALLPARK

Populous got its initial look at the Minneapolis Warehouse District site in March 2000, and first impressions weren't good. The first thing urban designer Kobi Bradley saw when he stepped from his downtown hotel was a trashcan blowing down the street in a gust of icy wind. Things only got worse after that. The site was just four blocks away, but after walking two blocks and reaching First Avenue, Bradley encountered a sidewalk that was all but disintegrated, and he found himself in a forbidding urban canyon. The piece of land in question was a surface parking lot crouching on the backside of Target Center. That was fine. But the sunken lot was surrounded by impediments that would make a ballpark difficult, if not impossible.

A freeway ran along the property's eastern side, and railroad tracks bordered on the west. Elevated streets hemmed in the lot to the north and south, making the challenges both horizontal and vertical. Moreover, the lot was small, as small as the properties in San Francisco and Pittsburgh that had proved minimal for major league layouts.

Then there was the neighborhood itself. Compared to the other cities that Bradley had scouted for sports venues, much of downtown Minneapolis seemed a gritty and desolate place, largely because an extensive system of second-story skyways took the vitality off the street level. There were few tree-lined sidewalks or storefronts to draw pedestrian interest. Walking around the ballpark area was particularly difficult because streets were designed exclusively for cars, and some lacked sidewalks altogether. Although a number of pricey condos were sprouting up nearby, and the shells of old brick warehouses were strikingly beautiful, the site's dominant neighbors were a giant garbage burner and a homeless shelter.

"Can't we find another site?" was the question on Bradley's lips when he returned to Kansas City. Plainly, this was not love at first sight.

"If this site had presented itself to me in another time and another place, I'm pretty sure I would have rejected it. It took six months to understand that there was a **glimmer** of hope."

—*Earl Santee, architect, Populous*

POTENTIAL WINS THE DAY

Despite its limitations, community leaders persisted in seeing big potential in the site. The lot was located at the confluence of at least five future rail transit lines. They envisioned the ballpark's playing field being elevated 30 feet, to the level of the Fifth and Seventh Street bridges. Trains could then run underneath the field, at ground level. The architects were amused by the idea. Yes, it was technically possible to build a stadium over a train station, but the cost would be stupendous.

Still, Minneapolis' relentless optimism impressed Santee and his staff, and like most good architects, they were game for a challenge. To add a dose of realism to the daunting project, they composed a list of 16 "fatal flaws" that any ballpark on the site would have to overcome. Failure to mitigate any of the 16 could kill the whole idea.

Among the 16:

- The ballpark, elevated or not, would have to be compatible with the converging train lines.
- Space would be needed for the Cedar Lake bike trail.
- Odors from trucks unloading at the neighboring trash burner (Hennepin Energy Recovery Center, or HERC) would have to be controlled.
- Air rights would have to be obtained for extending part of the stadium over Interstate 394 and part of the HERC property to accommodate the retractable roof structure.
- Railroad tracks along the project's west side would have to be moved 60 feet or more.

The last challenge would be a particularly tough one, since railroads are notoriously difficult negotiators, and no accommodation was assured.

The neighborhood's grim sidewalks would also have to be rehabbed with trees, better lighting, and other pedestrian amenities. "This was a big leap of faith for the Twins, for the city, and for us," Santee said.

"This was a big leap

of **faith** for the Twins,

for the city, and for us."

—*Earl Santee, architect, Populous*

Aerial view of the approved site with a digital rendering of the completed ballpark

The first sketches of Target Field. Although urban designer Kobi Bradley was initially unimpressed by the Warehouse District site, he sketched the first drawings of the ballpark on two hotel napkins in March 2000. Eventually, Bradley and others at Populous came to see the site as the ultimate urban ballpark challenge, and they took great pride in nestling the ballpark into the city.

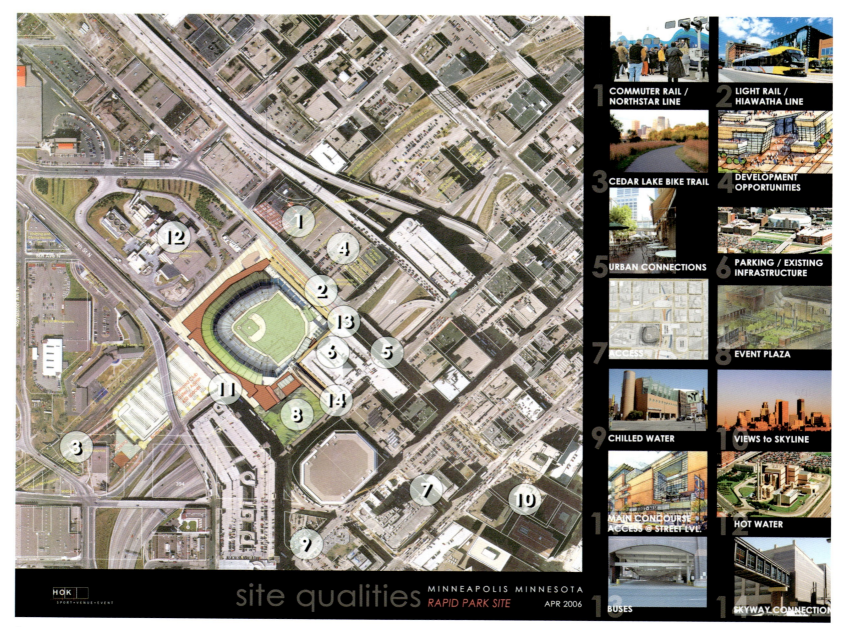

COMMUTER RAIL /
NORTHSTAR LINE

LIGHT RAIL /
HIAWATHA LINE

CEDAR LAKE BIKE TRAIL

DEVELOPMENT
OPPORTUNITIES

URBAN CONNECTIONS

PARKING / EXISTING
INFRASTRUCTURE

ACCESS

EVENT PLAZA

CHILLED WATER

VIEWS to SKYLINE

MAIN CONCOURSE
ACCESS @ STREET LVL.

HOT WATER

BUSES

SKYWAY CONNECTION

site qualities *RAPID PARK SITE*   MINNEAPOLIS MINNESOTA   APR 2006

Despite its challenges, the Rapid Park site also offered
many advantages for fans and the neighborhood.

Ironically, some of the site's biggest challenges were also its best attributes. Hundreds of millions of dollars in infrastructure were already in place. Two freeways ran nearby. Three immense parking ramps, three bus stations, and several skyway connections lay just beyond the outfield walls. New transit lines would deliver fans to within a few feet of the ballpark. Riding a bike to a game would be convenient and fun. Even the HERC could be turned into a "green" positive by delivering heat to the playing field, perhaps even to the seats. All those hot dog wrappers, drink cups, and peanut shells could be swept up after a game and pumped directly into the HERC for incineration. Within six blocks of the site, opportunities were flush for new housing, office, and retail construction. More than 200,000 downtown office workers, residents, and daily visitors were within easy walking distance, if attractive ways could be found to get pedestrians to a game.

88   CHAPTER 3

SQUARE PEG, ROUND HOLE

How best to fit a ballpark into this odd little gulch?

Santee quickly rejected an elevated playing field. Keeping the field down below the bridges would save money while also providing a hidden service level for loading docks, team clubhouses, and other back-of-the-house operations. That, in turn, would place the ballpark's main concourse even with the Fifth and Seventh Street bridges, allowing fans to step straight into the park, gaze down at the field, and walk down—not up—to their seats in the main bowl.

The next question: How should the field be oriented? To keep the setting sun out of a batter's eyes, home plate is nearly always placed on the west side of a ballpark. For Target Field, the southwest corner worked best for batters while also opening impressive skyline views for spectators. That put the main entrance not at home plate but in right field. In effect, a big "picture window" in right field would give entering fans a dramatic view of the ballpark interior, and give seated fans a dramatic view of the city. It was a win-win.

With the main entrance in right field, pedestrian access from Sixth Street drew particular attention. Designers envisioned a large plaza spanning the freeway to connect the ballpark to the heart of downtown. When that idea proved too costly, a narrow pedestrian bridge was considered. Ultimately the team formed a financial partnership with Target Corporation to fund the plaza concept, albeit on a smaller scale.

As in all ballparks, shadows and winds were also considered. Target Field is oriented so that seats along the first-base line are shady for day games, with shadows moving onto the field in late afternoon. Strong winds from the south often blow in the spring, which would make home runs to right field harder to hit. The opposite happens in late summer, however, when prevailing winds blow from the northwest out toward right field.

Hemmed in on all sides, the shape of the playing field and the configuration of the stands were dictated by urban surroundings, just as they were at Ebbets Field, Fenway Park, and all the classic urban ballparks. Because of the tight fit, foul territory at Target Field is smaller than at the Metrodome, and the outfield is a bit less roomy in left-center.

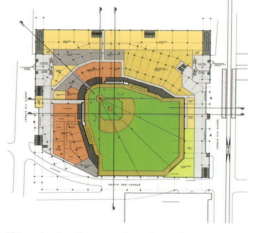

This early plan illustrates the tight configuration of the playing field within the urban setting. The design eventually called for building over the Third Avenue thoroughfare beyond right field.

Hemmed in on all sides,

the shape of the playing field and the configuration of the stands

were dictated by **urban surroundings**.

Baseball architects always fret over dimensions because the impact of distances and wind currents is notoriously tricky to predict. When the new Yankee Stadium opened in 2009, its right-field wall averaged only five feet closer to home plate than at the old stadium, located just next door, but subtly different wind currents turned the new park into a home run launching pad. At Target Field, architects swallowed hard and drew outfield dimensions comparable to major league averages—a bit larger than average in left and a bit smaller in right, but with a high wall. All in all, the new dimensions are almost identical to those at the Metrodome.

BALLPARK COMPARISON

Outfield Dimensions	Metrodome	Target Field
Left field	343 ft.	339 ft.
Left-center	385 ft.	377 ft.
Center field	408 ft.	404 ft.
Right-center	367 ft.	365 ft.
Right field	327 ft.	328 ft.
Foul territory	30,244 sq. ft.	22,042 sq. ft.
Wall Height		
Left field	7 ft.	8 ft.
Center field	7 ft.	8 ft.
Right field	23 ft.	23 ft.
Seating and Concourses		
Capacity (approx.)	55,300	39,504
Lower level	22,289	19,000
Upper level	32,445	13,000
Club level	n/a	7,000
Suites	95	54
Concourse width (main)	22 ft.	40 ft.
Concourse width (upper)	22 ft.	26–44 ft.
Restroom fixtures	256 (w), 192 (m)	401 (w), 266 (m)

Five Major League ballparks have less foul territory than Target Field: Fenway Park in Boston (19,083 square feet); Minute Maid Park in Houston (20,179); PNC Park in Pittsburgh (21,136); Camden Yards in Baltimore (21,306), and Progressive Field in Cleveland (21,455).

Two other ballparks, San Francisco's AT&T Park (22,369) and Chicago's Wrigley Field (22,485), have slightly more foul ground than Target Field.

Several variations for a bridge extension to connect the main right-field entrance with Sixth Street were considered, ranging from a vast plaza straddling Interstate 394 to a narrow pedestrian walkway.

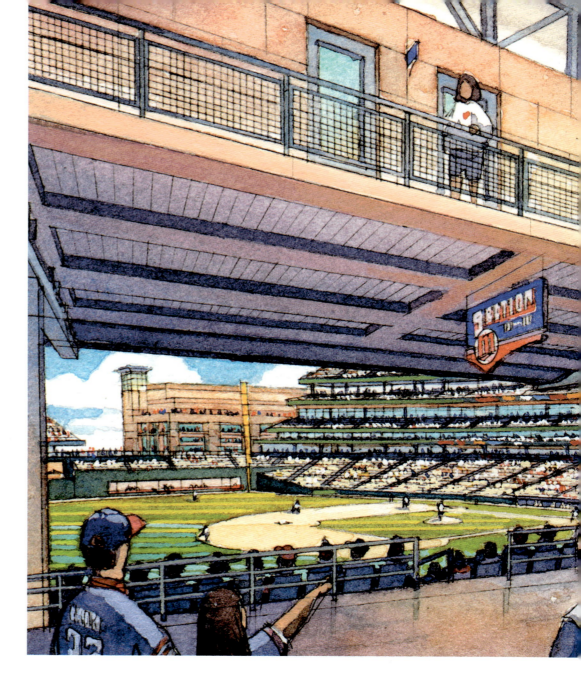

Although its design underwent several revisions, a main concourse that was open to the playing field was always an important consideration.

As for seating capacity, smaller was considered better. Many of the multipurpose stadiums built in the 1960s and 1970s boasted capacities that exceeded 60,000 and 70,000, mostly to accommodate pro football. The return to baseball-only layouts in the 1990s and 2000s provided fans with a more intimate experience. As of 2010, only 5 of the 30 major league venues contain more than 50,000 seats. In midsized markets like the Twin Cities, new ballparks aim to seat about 40,000. Avoiding the look—and the expense—of empty seats is a prime reason. Denver's Coors Field, which has a capacity of 50,445 and where the right-field upper deck is routinely empty, is often cited as a lesson. In the Denver market, slightly smaller than Minneapolis–St. Paul, a ballpark can't justify 50,000 seats.

At Target Field, as was done at small-footprint stadiums in San Francisco and Pittsburgh, the architects had to stack nearly all the seating between the foul poles—not a bad thing for spectators. Designers devised six levels, each connected to a wide main concourse that runs the full 360 degrees of the ballpark and offers open views to the playing field.

The Twins wanted an **intimate** seating bowl and an open, 360-degree view of the field.

The **Event (or Service) Level** is roughly even with the playing field and features an exclusive seating area behind home plate. It also includes loading docks, food service operations, back-of-the-house staging areas, player clubhouses, and dugouts.

Most fans enter at the **Main Concourse**, located at the top of the lower seating bowl. This level contains nearly half of the ballpark's total seats. Seats extend nearly down to field level, on a rake considerably less steep than the Metrodome's. The design places fans extremely close to the action.

A **Club Level** cantilevers over part of the lower bowl. Some fans pay premium prices to sit on this level because it includes access to the Delta SKY360 Legends Club climate-controlled amenities, which are located adjacent to their seats.

The **Suite Level** is perched above the Club Level. Suites, often purchased by corporations, resemble indoor/outdoor lofts with kitchen areas and both indoor and outdoor seating overlooking the field. Flat-screen TVs and catered food are part of the package.

The upper deck contains two levels—the **Terrace and View levels**—sharing a common concourse. Together they form one of the smallest upper decks in the major leagues. The press box, originally planned for the center of the View Level, was moved down two decks to the Club Level.

Main Concourse Level

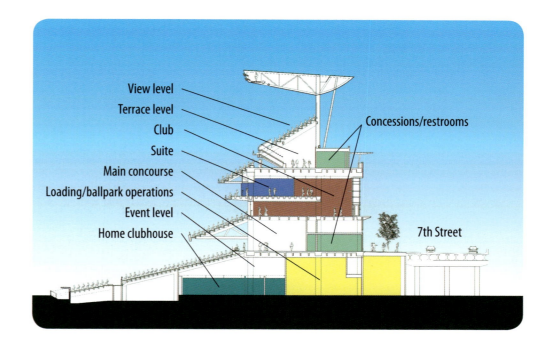

THE SIX LEVELS OF TARGET FIELD

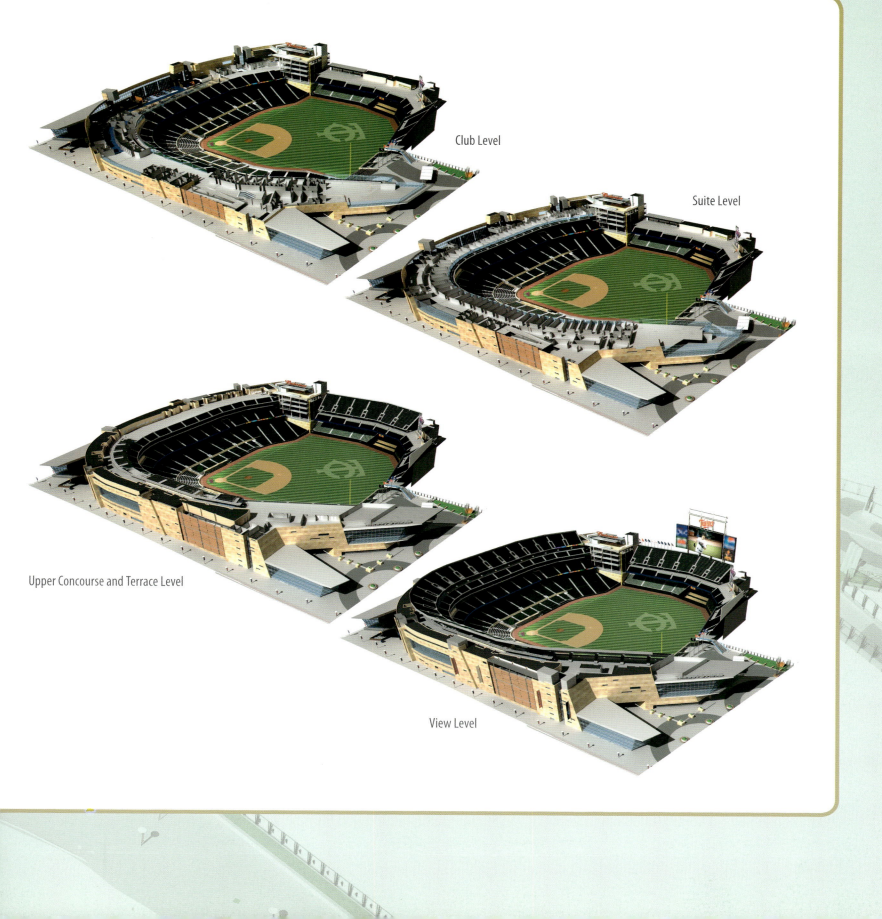

Club Level

Suite Level

Upper Concourse and Terrace Level

View Level

A generation of fans,

with no memory of

outdoor baseball,

would have to adjust.

TO ROOF OR NOT TO ROOF—THAT WAS THE QUESTION

In the Minneapolis–St. Paul market, the question of a roof has meaning beyond baseball. It is a matter of outlook: Is life filled mostly with hostile conditions, requiring protection from cold, wind, heat, bugs, and other vicissitudes? Or is life filled with the possibility of fine days and the willingness to embrace whatever comes?

Comfort and practicality drive those in the first camp. Given an opportunity to see a game, the pragmatist's instinct is to ask, "What if it's cold and rainy?" The second camp holds out for the promise of sunny days and perfect summer nights under the stars. Idealism drives these people. They see every glass as half full.

Given this split personality, the Twins regarded a retractable roof as the fairest solution. For a generation, the Metrodome had provided fans throughout the Upper Midwest with a guarantee that they would see baseball on any weekend trip to the Twin Cities. Retractable

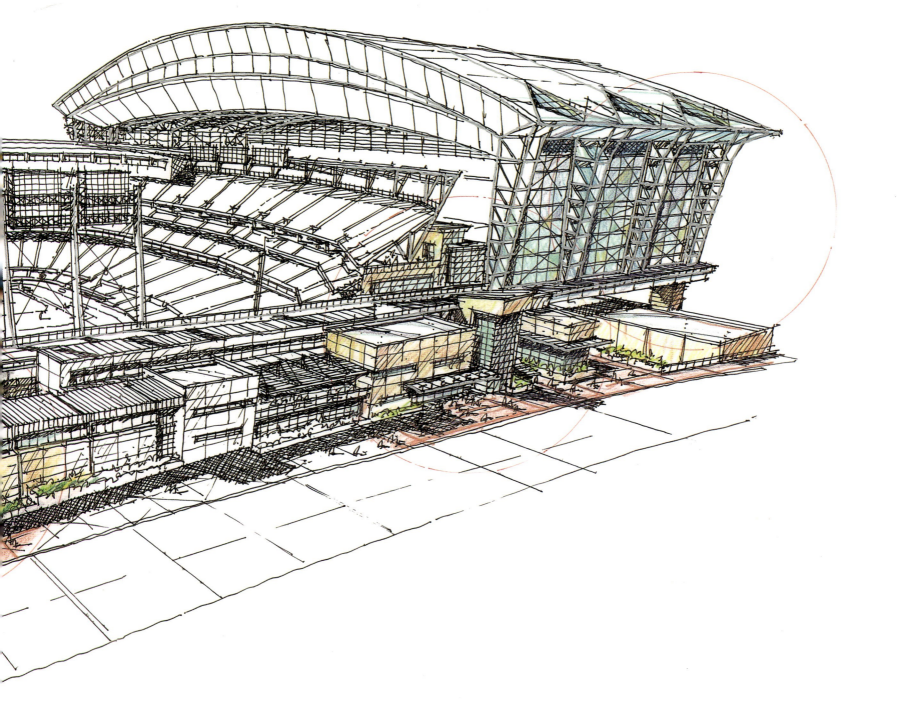

roofs in Milwaukee, Toronto, Seattle, Phoenix, and Houston were giving those fans the best of both worlds, so why not here? The team did not foresee a true indoor/outdoor stadium but rather a lid that would slide over the field during rainy weather, as architects had designed in Seattle. For fans, the experience would be a lot like sitting under a big umbrella.

Trouble was, the umbrella would cost $130 million. The team felt it could not afford a roof without a big hike in ticket prices. The Hennepin County commissioners saw no need for a roof; if outstate fans wanted a roof, they could convince the state government to pay for one. The state, after all, hadn't spent a nickel on the project. The state legislature showed no interest, however, and the idea for the roof was dropped. A generation of fans, with no memory of outdoor baseball, would have to adjust to the potentially chilly, windy days of April, May, and October, the rainstorms of June and July, and the gorgeous sunshine and moonlight of August and September.

A retractable roof was part of some early design plans, but the costs and the limitations to the design proved prohibitive. The roof mechanism dominated the overall design, creating a hangar-like extension on the third-base side.

Never before have

Major League Baseball fans

been asked to change from

a totally indoor environment

to a **totally outdoor** one.

In fact, Twin Cities temperatures and rainfall amounts during baseball season are comparable to those of other northern cities.

The Twins expect three or four rainouts during an average season and a similar number of games during which rainstorms will delay play. One happy result, however, is that doubleheaders have returned to the Twin Cities sports schedule for the first time in three decades. As for cold weather, radiant heat was added to the concourses, restrooms, and concessions areas to provide some refuge.

Still, no one underestimates the adjustment. Never before have Major League Baseball fans been asked to change from a totally indoor environment to a totally outdoor one. (Indoor-only stadiums in Houston and Seattle—the Astrodome and Kingdome—were replaced by ballparks with retractable roofs.)

The proposed retractable roof would have extended over the field on tracks running along the first-base side and beyond left field, covering but not fully enclosing the stadium.

Average Temperature	April	May	June	July	August	September	Season Average Temperature	Season Average Rainfall
Chicago	49	59	69	73	72	64	64.3	22.44
Boston	48	58	68	74	72	65	64.1	19.08
Detroit	47	48	58	72	71	63	63.1	18.98
Twin Cities	46	59	68	74	71	61	63.1	19.73
Toronto*	46	58	67	72	70	63	62.6	16.70
Milwaukee*	44	55	65	71	69	62	61.0	19.96
Seattle*	50	56	61	65	66	61	59.8	9.95

*Retractable-roof stadium

"We wanted to find the **magic**."

The elimination of the roof allowed the designers to pursue a more graceful, compact, and streamlined look to the ballpark's profile.

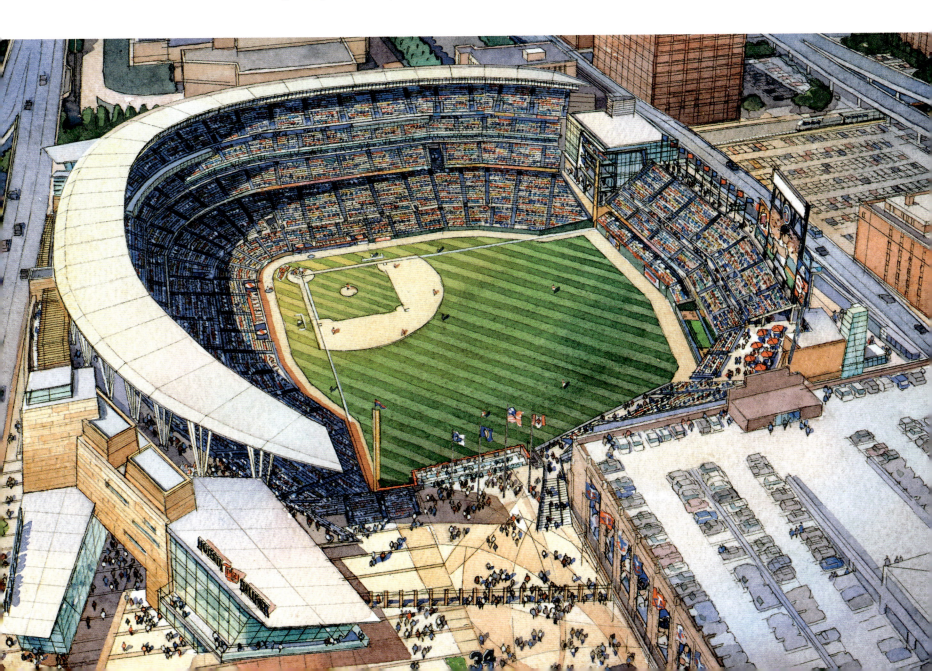

SEARCHING FOR ARCHITECTURAL POETRY

Designers were not unhappy about the decision to drop the roof. A stadium roof structure, complete with supporting columns and elevated tracks, is a massive thing. It dominates a building. It lessens the chance for graceful design. It overwhelms the scale of any neighborhood. Target Field's roof, in nice weather, would have been stored over the top of the HERC property. On rainy days it would have glided on elevated tracks toward right field. It would have required towering supports 30 feet thick and 150 feet tall. A roofed ballpark would have loomed over the Warehouse District like a brooding airplane hangar.

Without a roof, architects were free to pursue a design guided purely by aesthetics. Several approaches were considered: a retro-styled building of red brick to match others in the Warehouse District; a building of stone arches to recall historic Mississippi River bridges; or something sleek and modern, in scale with the surroundings but set apart in its design.

"There was an evolution in our thinking," said Jim Pohlad. "We ended up wanting something distinctive that didn't look like another retro ballpark." Pohlad in particular among the Twins' top management was keen on creating a modern building that would uniquely celebrate Minnesota, one that, when seen by a national TV audience, would evoke the beauty of the state's natural features yet capture a sophisticated urban context. People from all over would know that they were looking at Minneapolis.

Indeed, the site seemed to dictate a forward-looking building. The links to rail transit, walking and biking access, and other green features, plus an expectation that the ballpark would help generate dense and lively urban living around it, fit the tone of the times.

In September 2006, Populous invited team executives, community leaders, representatives from Mortenson Construction, and fellow architects from Minneapolis-based partner HGA to its studio in lower Manhattan to push the creativity envelope on the ballpark's look and feel. "We wanted to find the magic," Santee recalled.

The three-day charette—an intensive period of design discussion and planning—produced a gush of ideas inspired by Minnesota's natural features and architectural context. Sky-tinted waters, rocky cliffs, stone ledges and outcroppings, ice crystals, pine forests, grassy prairies, and dramatic skies were considered. So were vernacular buildings and local landmarks, including Cesar Pelli's Minneapolis Central Library, the Stone Arch Bridge, and the WCCO television headquarters on Nicollet Mall, admired for its golden limestone exterior. "We always had the idea of native stone," Santee said. "It is so beautiful."

Incorporating those themes and influences into the ballpark generated a multitude of design ideas; some were bizarre and fanciful, others would become important pieces of the ballpark's identity. A distinctive character was beginning to emerge.

A variety of local-Minnesota architectural and natural features were used as inspiration during the charette.

Carl Pohlad and other team executives and community leaders joined architects and designers to brainstorm ideas at a three-day charette in New York.

THE MINNESOTA TWINS DESIGN CHARETTE

LETTING THE IMAGINATION RUN WILD is an important part of the design process. From September 12 through 14, 2006, Populous invited Twins representatives, architects from Minneapolis-based HGA, and Twin Cities community leaders to its New York studio to explore creative ideas that might raise the ballpark's design to new levels. The intent was to find a distinctive character, a bit of poetry, for the project. A slew of fanciful ideas were proposed but ultimately rejected, including cables to support the lights and canopy, a waterfall in center field, and a dramatic wedge-shaped administrative building. The most tempting new idea called for stylish 300-foot towers to be built as foul poles, but they were discarded for cost reasons. Of the ideas that survived, the crescent-shaped canopy emerged as the ballpark's most striking feature. Following are some of the sketches generated by the charette.

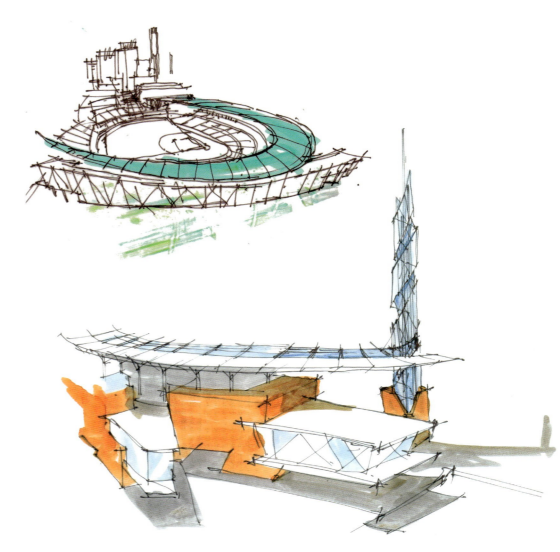

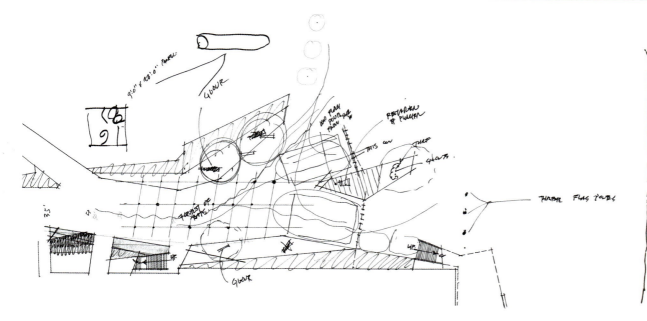

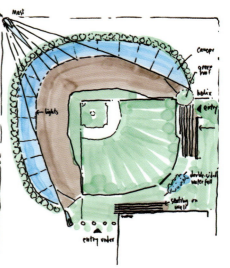

ENTRY.

ENTRY

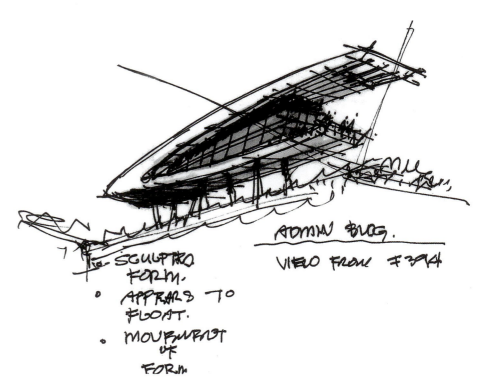

ADMIN BLDG.

VIEW FROM #3904

• SCULPTED FORM.
• APPEARS TO FLOAT.
• MOVEMENT OF FORM

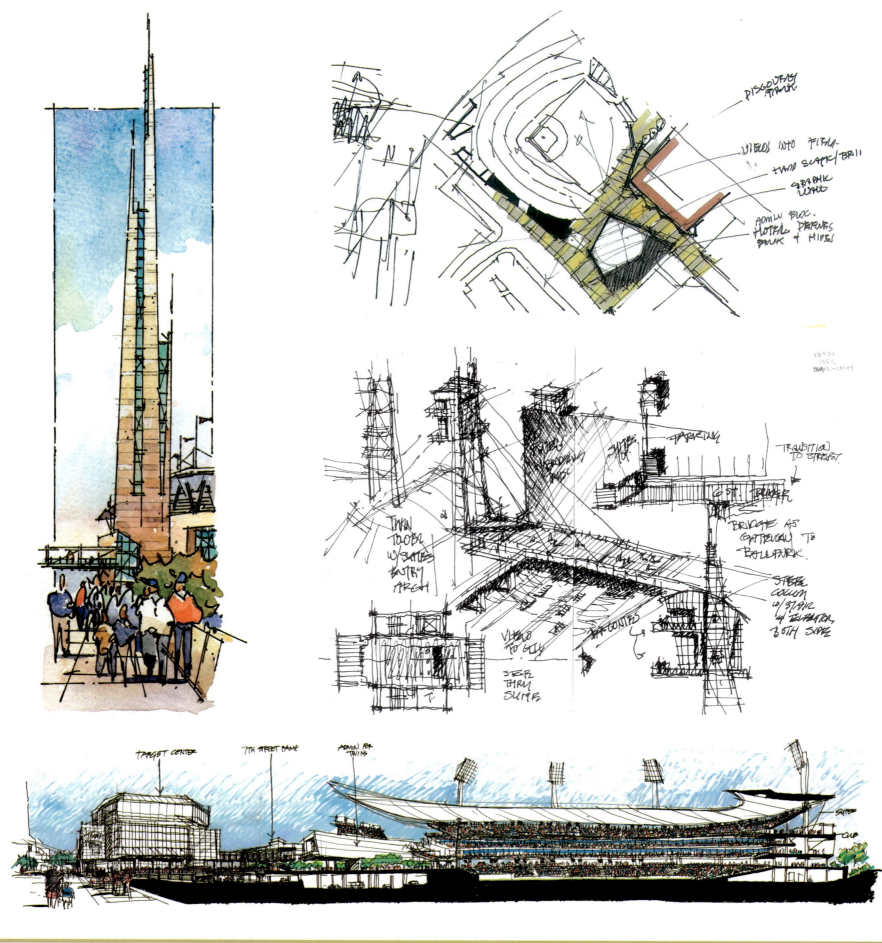

DISCOVERY PARK

VIEWS INTO FIELD

LANDSCAPE/TRAIL

GRAPHIC WALL

ADMIN BLDG
HOTEL DEFINES
PARK & MIDE

TRADITION
TO STREET

MAIN TOWER
W/SUITES
ENTRY
AREA

SHOP

PARKING

BRIDGE AS
GATEWAY TO
BALLPARK.

BRIDGE

STEEL
COLUMN
W/STAIR
& ELEVATOR
BOTH SIDE

VIDEO
TO GIU

RACONTR

SEE
THRU
SLIDE

TARGET CENTER   7TH STREET BANK   ADMIN FOR TWINS

SUITE

CLUB

VIDEO
TO GIU

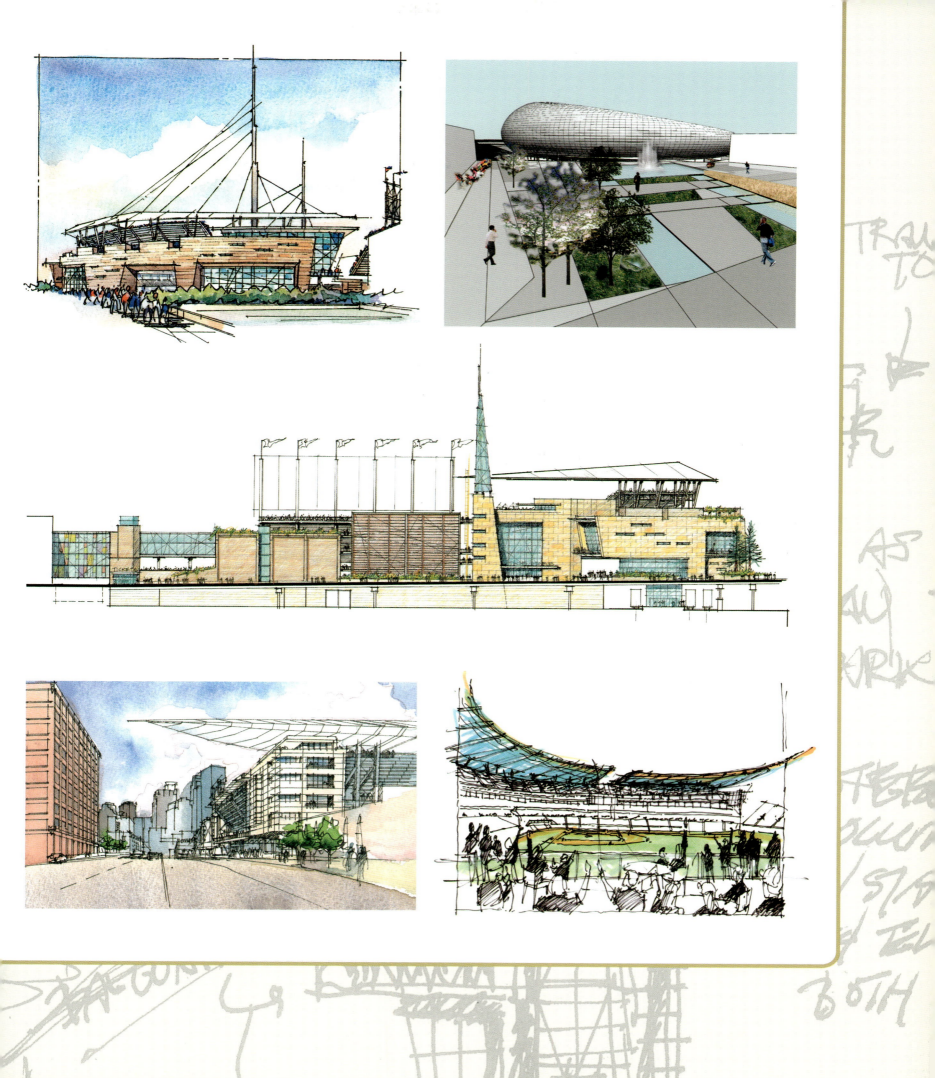

Before: Initial designs placed the scoreboard and team offices in right field, blocking any visual pathway to the downtown core. (Note that the artist shifted the city skyline toward center field in this rendering.)

FINDING A DISTINCTIVE CHARACTER

With a footprint of only one million square feet, the ballpark's layout allowed limited space for outfield seating, making the look and feel of the outfield backdrop particularly important. The design was juggled several times to try to artfully frame the structure's north and east sides while opening up views and access to downtown. Twins owner and CEO Jim Pohlad, joined by Ballpark Authority Director Dan Kenney, urged that the team-office wing, which dominated the right-field vistas in early designs, be relocated to allow for a larger plaza, better views, and a seamless connection to the downtown core.

The architects complied by moving both the office wing and the scoreboard from right field to left. It was an important step that began to give the project a distinct personality. Team president Dave St. Peter called it a "light-bulb moment for the Twins." Only by imagining what it would be like to stand on the plaza could you appreciate its critical function as a connector of the ballpark to the city. At least two-thirds of fans were expected

After: Moving the offices and scoreboard to left field opened up the plaza and offered a direct connection to the city center. The large batter's eye restaurant was eventually dropped from center field.

to enter through the two gates in right field. Another quarter were expected to use the two gates in left field, near the light-rail station, with only a few entering near home plate.

The team decided that each of the five gates would carry the retired number of a legendary Twins player: Gates 34 and 29 off the right-field plaza for Kirby Puckett and Rod Carew; Gates 3 and 6 in left field for Harmon Killebrew and Tony Oliva; and Gate 14 at home plate for Kent Hrbek.

As the architects explored the various concepts in the months following the charette, the overall look and feel of the ballpark continued to evolve. Some big ideas were dropped or modified. Two thin towers at the foul poles were eliminated for cost reasons. A waterfall in center field was similarly abandoned. Condos in left field (the North Star Flats) and a "Batter's Eye" club in center field were omitted. Cables to support light standards and the canopy were discarded. The hopes of heating seats or pumping trash to the HERC were dashed because of technical, cost, and labor difficulties.

CONCEIVING TARGET PLAZA

IT WAS OBVIOUS EARLY IN THE DESIGN PROCESS that the main entrance to the Twins' new ballpark should be in right field. But there was one huge problem: a recessed freeway (Interstate 394) ran precisely where the entrance needed to be.

The solution was a plaza that would stretch over the top of the freeway to form a front porch for the ballpark as well as a festive gathering place for fans and a seamless connection to the heart of downtown. When initial plaza designs failed to excite Twins officials, they approached Oslund and Associates, an acclaimed Minneapolis landscape design firm noted for its artistic flair. Tom Oslund said he worried that his ideas would be "too abstract for the baseball guys," but he quickly won them over. It's not just the ballpark that's important, he told them, it's how people anticipate the ballpark and how the ballpark and the community flow into one another.

Indeed, the image of ancient water carving pathways in and out of a rocky primordial canyon is how Oslund first imagined the plaza. The ballpark, with its rugged stonework, was the canyon, and the fans were the streams of water flowing in and out. Oslund saw the plaza as the streambed, the conveyance that made the ballpark work.

It was the plaza, after all, flowing all the way from right field to First Avenue, that brought the ballpark to downtown's door-step. Even on days when no games were played, the space could emerge as a downtown focal point. But the design challenge was formidable: How to transform a stark layer of concrete spread over the top of a freeway into a beautiful green space where plants would thrive and visitors would be comfortable, whether alone or surrounded by 40,000 others?

Oslund decided to intersperse abstract baseball elements into the plaza's flow: a lineup of 40-foot topiaries that resemble baseball bats, circular planting beds the same size as pitcher's mounds, curved planters that mimic the stitching on a baseball, covered benches that look like cap visors, and an oversized bronze baseball glove. A wall commemorating Twins fans and teams of the past would be a part of the design, as would bronze sculptures of Harmon Killebrew, Rod Carew, and Kirby Puckett.

Most impressive, perhaps, was the huge kinetic wind sculpture covering an adjoining parking ramp. This veil, composed of metal flaps the size of baseball cards, would undulate in the wind to create a wavy, watery effect. It would become the largest piece of public art in the Twin Cities.

Grasping the opportunity to sponsor a major public plaza, Target Corporation joined with the Twins to fund the $8.5 million enterprise. Subtle "targets" replaced waves on the plaza's pavement.

For Oslund, the plaza's mission is to use design as a way to change social habits. "The whole notion of a baseball game has changed," he said. "Now it's about the total experience and inviting people to get out and enjoy their city."

The plaza design incorporated greenery in the topiaries as well as in the shaded seating area

Ground-level view showing the donor panels and wall dedicated to Twins history (on the right) as well as the topiary frames, bronze baseball glove, and large wind sculpture in the background

Overhead view of the final design plan for Target Plaza

KEY

1 mound planters
2 topiary frames
3 Target logo
4 The Golden Glove
5 shade canopies (visors)
6 Gate 34
7 Target logo paving pattern
8 raised turf areas
9 vending cart locations
10 wind veil
11 skyway
12 stairs to plaza from skyway
13 stairs to outfield upper deck seating
14 ticketing area
15 ticket office
16 pro shop
17 drop-off area
18 Kirby Puckett statue
19 Harmon Killebrew statue
20 Rod Carew statue
21 Minnesota Ballpark History Monument
22 skyway tower
23 6th Street pedestrian extension

Although the large, free-standing numbers were eventually eliminated, the idea to number the gates after the team's five retired jersey numbers brings a distinctly Twins flavor.

The team decided that each of the five gates would carry the **retired number** of a legendary Twins player.

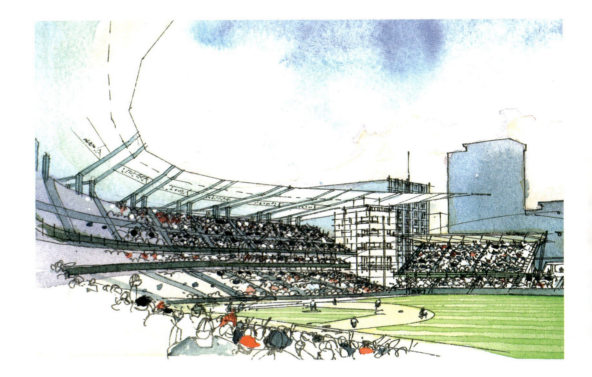

Right: A canopy over the upper deck, originally displaying a bat-wing-like design, was another defining concept to emerge from the charette.

Opposite: Among the ideas that ended up on the cutting-room floor were a large waterfall feature in center field and new condo construction beyond left field.

Among the most significant design evolutions was the dramatic canopy, which would appear to hover above the upper deck. "Floating clouds above water" was how Kobi Bradley described the inspiration. Not only would the canopy be visually stunning, it would reflect sound back down to the field to enhance a lively atmosphere.

In the aftermath of the charette, the canopy's look transformed from a bat-winged appearance to a more graceful crescent. Lights were embedded into the canopy itself, eliminating the need for light towers. The effect was stunning and unprecedented. The ballpark's overall profile was lowered, and it took on a streamlined look. The canopy, with its glowing crescent of lights, was set atop what appeared to be bundles of sticks (or perhaps icicles) that protruded upward from a rocky outcropping. Parts of the stone structure jutted dramatically outward from its main mass to house glassed-in restaurants and a retail store. The ballpark seemed finally to have developed a character all its own.

Not only would the canopy be visually stunning,

it would reflect sound back down to the field

to enhance a **lively** atmosphere.

The ballpark

seemed finally

to have developed

a **character**

all its own.

The canopy, with its embedded lights, assumed a more streamlined profile as the design was refined, making it an even more distinctive characteristic.

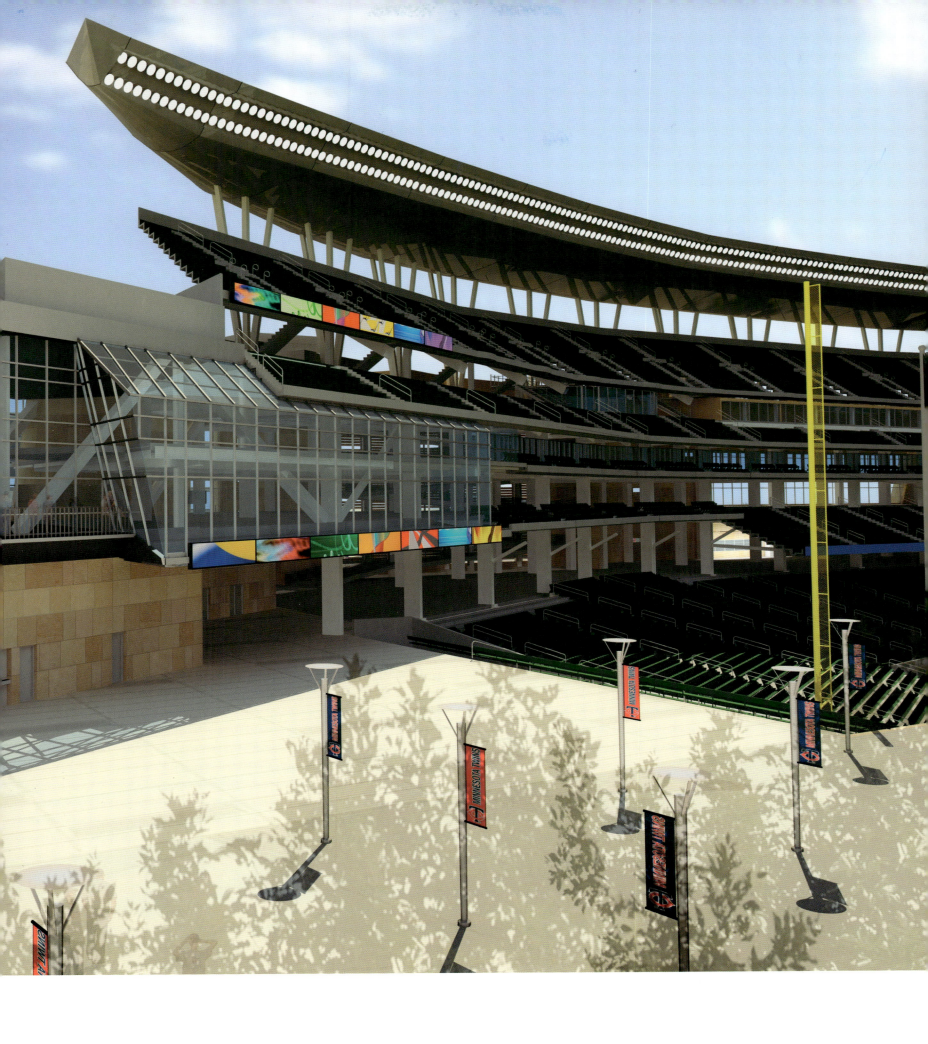

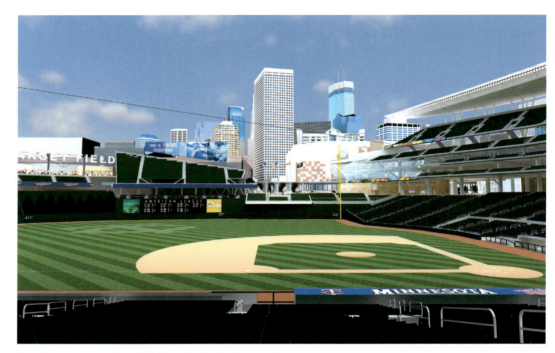

The signature view of Target Field—distinctly Minneapolis

The seats would be green, the color of summer and a nice contrast to the golden limestone exterior. An intimate, double-decked porch in left field contributed to the ballpark's cozy atmosphere, and a small grandstand in right-center served to hide a parking deck. The bullpens were cut into the left-field porch at field level, instead of being placed along the foul lines, as in the Metrodome. Next to the bullpens, native black spruce trees were planted to form a hitter's backdrop (batter's eye) in center field. At the end of the right-field plaza, which extended to the very edge of the playing field, a small overhang filled with flowers cantilevered over a portion of the outfield. The overhang is capable of snatching a deep fly ball from the grasp of a right fielder waiting below. Balls might also ricochet off the stone-covered overhang at unpredictable angles. This was the only slight contrivance in an otherwise classic layout. The Twins didn't want gimmicks.

The Pohlad family chose to spend beyond its $130 million portion of the ballpark's cost—more than $55 million extra—in order to enhance the design. The handsome canopy was one addition. Stone, and lots of it, was added to the interior to provide a refined look. Radiant heat was provided to afford fans more comfort on chilly days. Classic wood-back seats were selected to upgrade the Club Level. And the latest Internet television technology was installed throughout the building. Extra money also went into improving the pedestrian atmosphere in the blocks surrounding Target Field. "The Pohlad family took a good ballpark and made it a great one," Santee said.

"The Pohlad family took a good ballpark and made it a **great** one."

—*Earl Santee, architect, Populous*

HOW MUCH ADVERTISING?

LONG BEFORE MEGABUCKS DOMINATED BASEBALL, advertising dominated ballparks—lots of advertising. The outfield walls of the old urban stadiums were plastered with signboards. Gem razor blades and Schaeffer beer were embedded into Brooklyn's fabled Ebbets Field. A Longines clock and a giant Chesterfield cigarette (with smoke) overlooked the Polo Grounds in Manhattan. The big Citgo sign still looming over Fenway Park has become part of Boston lore.

Some modern-day ballparks are so saturated with advertisements and electronic billboards that they almost overwhelm the action on the field. Chicago's Wrigley Field is one of the few ballparks that downplays advertising. With walls covered in ivy instead of signage, it feels as much like a park as a ballpark.

The Twins aimed for a happy medium at Target Field. "We think that the ballpark itself is so visually impressive that people don't need or want the extra stimulation," Twins President Dave St. Peter said. "We want fans to have fun, and we have a number of advertising signs. But our hope is to emphasize the ballpark and the classic experience."

BREAKING AWAY FROM THE ORDINARY

The Twins' new home mixes modern frills with the intimacy of bygone ballparks, just as Camden Yards did in the early 1990s—but Target Field breaks away from what has become a cliché in ballpark construction. There's no retro to its style. Its lines are modern, sleek, and sophisticated enough to place it legitimately among the Guthrie Theater, Walker Art Center, and Minneapolis Central Library as iconic symbols of Minneapolis' cultural renewal of the early twenty-first century. The craggy limestone exterior, punctured by icy glass openings, evokes Minnesota's river bluffs and North Shore cliffs. Its elegant canopy, a glowing crescent of lights that seems to float above the seating bowl, is unlike anything in any American city. The cozy ambience and seamless connections to its surroundings make Target Field a truly urban ballpark. Taken all together, Target Field has a chance to achieve crossover appeal: sports architecture as art.

"That will be for the critics to decide," said Santee.

"Target Field is not about the last century; it's about the **next** century."

—Dan Kenney, director of the Minnesota Ballpark Authority

"It's a warm and interesting building. It's small, but the proportions are right. It's not overstated or understated. It developed over a period of seven or eight years, so it feels organic, not forced. . . . It came out of nothing to become something. It shows how a building form **connects** to the city."

—*Earl Santee, architect, Populous*

An architect can't help but have personal feelings toward his projects, even if they don't match the firm's official corporate neutrality on such matters. Architecture is full of personal emotion, Santee acknowledged. Everyone who has worked on the project feels an emotional bond. For Santee and his design team, Target Field is special for many reasons. "It's a beautiful building," he said. "It's at the top of the list."

One curiosity about Target Field is that the viewer can never catch a glimpse of the whole structure. You can be walking or driving a block or two away and have no clue it's there. Like the ballparks built nearly a century ago, it is set so intimately into the grid of the city that you happen upon it only when turning a corner and—pow! There it is! That's precisely the point of the building, Santee explained. Target Field is inseparable from the city that surrounds it. It's a built-in ballpark.

Another reason it succeeds architecturally, Santee said, is that it "had a long time to marinate" in the minds of designers—so much so that it appears to have been drawn by a single hand even though 130 architects took part. The end result "fits the Twins and the city like a glove," Santee said. His hope is that Minnesotans fall in love with the place as much as its designers have, although true affection for ballparks typically accumulates over years, sometimes decades. Baseball is about memories.

Above: Elements of Target Field peak out from between buildings and above the skyways of downtown Minneapolis, making it feel like it was custom fit for the city.

Add all of that rail activity to the convergence

of buses, bikes, freeways, and decked parking spots,

and you get a major **Transportation Interchange**.

GETTING IN AND OUT Target Field as Transit Hub

SUCCESSFUL URBAN BALLPARKS ARE DEFINED BY THE "TOTAL EXPERIENCE," including the options they provide for getting in and out of the stadium area. Target Field's location offers plenty of choices. Two major freeways and a grid of streets surround the site. More than 7,000 parking spots are located in three big ramps just beyond the outfield walls, and 20,000 more are available within a three-quarter-mile walk.

More than 20 metro bus lines run out of stations in the A and B parking ramps, and Minneapolis' main intercity bus terminal adjoins the A ramp.

Target Plaza gives pedestrians a straight shot to and from the downtown core, either on street-level sidewalks or through the skyway system. The Cedar Lake Trail, part of an extensive bicycle network, runs through a tunnel beneath the ballpark. Several hundred bike racks are nearby. About the only transportation choice not considered was a ferry dock on the Mississippi River six blocks away.

Perhaps the most notable options are the light-rail and commuter-rail platforms located just steps from the ballpark's gates.

The idea of a ballpark sharing space with rail transit isn't altogether new to Minnesota. Nicollet Park, home of the Minneapolis Millers from 1896 to 1955, sat next to the "car barns" of the old Twin City Rapid Transit Company at Nicollet Avenue and Thirty-first Street South. Riding a streetcar to the game was a common practice. Indeed, riding streetcars between Nicollet Park and Lexington Park for July 4 doubleheaders between the Millers and St. Paul Saints was a ritual. So, in some sense, Target Field has brought Twin Cities baseball fans full circle.

Hiawatha light-rail trains run just beyond the left-field wall and connect the ballpark to downtown, the airport, and Bloomington. Northstar Commuter Rail trains run on a lower level, connecting the ballpark to Big Lake (and eventually St. Cloud). Other train lines are expected to follow: the Central light-rail line to the University and St. Paul; the Southwest and Bottineau lines to the southwest and northwest suburbs; the Northern Lights Express to Duluth; the Red Rock commuter line to Hastings; and perhaps, a high-speed connection to Chicago.

Add all of that rail activity to the convergence of buses, bikes, freeways, and decked parking spots, and you get a major Transportation Interchange expected to handle 22,000 trips per day within six years of Target Field's opening. And that doesn't count 8,000 extra trips on game days.

4

BALLPARK RISING

Constructing a Classic

"From the standpoint of the site,

this is the **most challenging project** we've ever built,

and I think the architect would say the same."

—Dan Mehls, construction executive, Mortenson Construction

The Target Field construction site was bustling through all seasons and all times of day to ensure that the challenging project was completed on schedule.

CONSTRUCTING TARGET FIELD WAS A GROUNDBREAKING ACHIEVEMENT in more than the literal sense.

Twelve acres of ballpark—minimal for a major league layout—had to be shoehorned into an eight-and-a-half-acre site. That meant the structure had to overlap its immediate surroundings, similar to the way a muffin overlaps its baking cup. The ballpark had to lean out over the top of a freeway and a railroad while protruding beneath two city streets and a light-rail line. The left-field grandstand had to double as a transit station, and the entire project had to function as a pedestrian bridge connecting a growing residential neighborhood to the downtown core.

That's a lot for one ballpark to accomplish.

Target Field's world-class designers and builders called the job the most challenging they had ever tackled—and, in the end, the most satisfying. The complexity of the task and the stunning result make the project a candidate for awards in the architectural and engineering world. The project offers a case study for transforming an extremely tight urban site into an extraordinary civic asset. Especially in the early twenty-first century, as the nation strives to rediscover life on a smaller footprint, the ballpark's construction techniques demonstrate the retrofitting of an old city for lively new purposes.

"It's the most **complex** design we've done

and the most **urban** of all the ballparks we've built."

—*Bruce Miller, project architect, Populous*

The ballpark's site was a challenge because of its tight fit, but thanks to the ingenuity of the designers and construction team, Target Field was completed ahead of schedule and under budget.

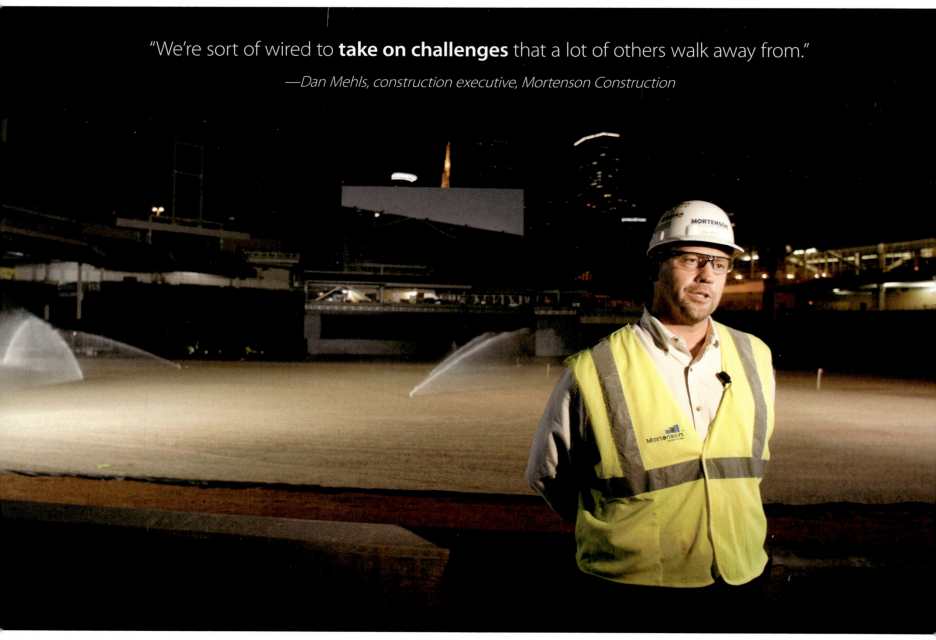

"We're sort of wired to **take on challenges** that a lot of others walk away from."

—*Dan Mehls, construction executive, Mortenson Construction*

Dan Mehls of Mortenson Construction

Michael Cuddyer, Joe Mauer, and Justin Morneau show up at the construction site equipped with their tools—to film a television ad in September 2007.

In that sense, Target Field is probably the most significant, and certainly the most urban, of the 20 or so ballparks built during the ballpark revival period that began in 1992. Several of those structures were built to help rejuvenate shabby waterfronts or warehouse districts; Baltimore's Oriole Park at Camden Yards, San Francisco's AT&T Park, and Denver's Coors Field are models for that. But others didn't accomplish much in the urban-design sense. New ballparks in Milwaukee, Atlanta, and Philadelphia, for example, were built amid roomy surface parking lots of the kind found in suburbia. No construction miracles were required. Even the new Yankee Stadium, although spectacular, was less a feat of engineering than an expression of excess and luxury. It was merely the best stadium that money could buy.

Target Field accomplishes far more in less space and for less money. No other ballpark of its generation overcame so many complications or required so much coordination among so many layers of government and private players. The very constraints that made Target Field such a tight fit delivered its greatest benefit: It is not just a new home for the Twins but a public plaza, a transit hub, a bike trail, and a retail center. And, because it doubles as a beautiful pedestrian bridge over what used to be an ugly trench, the ballpark will be a catalyst for neighborhood business, housing, and new development in the years ahead.

The daunting construction task fell to Mortenson Construction, a Minneapolis-based firm with a national reputation for taking on tough jobs. "We're sort of wired to take on challenges that a lot of others walk away from," said Dan Mehls, the company's construction executive for the ballpark. In addition to Mortenson's notable cultural and civic construction projects on both the local and national scene—from the Frank Gehry–designed Walt Disney Concert Hall in Los Angeles to the Minneapolis Central Library—the firm's portfolio also features a number of high-profile sports venues, including Xcel Energy Center in St. Paul and TCF Bank Stadium in Minneapolis. Mortenson is the nation's third largest sports contractor.

"They have extremely smart people, and they're on the leading edge of a lot of new construction technology," said Jerry Bell, president of Twins Sports Inc. The company's experience and its Twin Cities roots were big factors in its selection for the job, Bell said, adding, "We wanted as much of the project as possible to be done by Minnesota companies."

"We've never worked with a **classier** group of people than the Twins. Their handshake is as good as a contract. That's been the highlight of this experience."

—John Wood, principal in charge of the ballpark project, Mortenson Construction

MORTENSON CONSTRUCTION

MORTENSON CONSTRUCTION WAS FOUNDED IN 1954, but the family's roots in the construction trade go back to the nineteenth century.

Soon after Nels Mortenson left Sweden for the United States in 1897, he landed a job as a carpenter in Minneapolis. By 1924, he was a construction supervisor working on Memorial Stadium at the University of Minnesota. His ideas for more efficiently mixing and moving concrete around the site helped his employer to finish the stadium in just seven months—42 days ahead of schedule. His oldest son, Mort, worked as a carpenter's apprentice on the project.

Three years later, Nels Mortenson repeated his success in Ann Arbor by helping to build the University of Michigan's legendary football stadium. All three of his sons worked on the project, but it was Mort who was destined to make construction a family-owned business.

In 1954, with the postwar housing boom in full stride, Mort set out on his own. His first job was a $370 remodeling project for the Paul Bunyan Bait Company, but bigger jobs soon followed. By 1960, the new company had built Swedish Hospital, two Minneapolis churches, and a string of other projects. The Mortenson profile grew over the next decade as Mort's son, Mort Jr., led the company. Schools, hospitals, power plants, university buildings, and downtown office towers followed. By the turn of the twenty-first century, it was hard to go anywhere in the Twin Cities without seeing Mortenson's handiwork: Fairview Southdale Hospital, the Humphrey Institute at the University of Minnesota, the Minneapolis Convention Center, the Minneapolis Institute of Art, the Wells Fargo Tower, Xcel Energy Center, Walker Art Center, and the Minneapolis Central Library, just to name a few.

The company also won projects around the country, including numerous major sports and cultural venues: the Denver Art Museum and Coors Field in Denver; Edward Jones Dome in St. Louis; Sprint Center in Kansas City; FedEx Forum in Memphis; and the Marcus Center for the Performing Arts in Milwaukee. The firm's masterpiece is the Walt Disney Concert Hall in Los Angeles, a complex structure designed by renowned architect Frank Gehry and completed in 2003. It was a chance for Mortenson to show off its mastery of computer-aided construction, a skill the company further developed on the challenging Target Field project.

Despite advanced technology, Mortenson's projects are still driven by face-to-face human contacts. "We admire Mortenson for that," said Jerry Bell, president of Twins Sports Inc. "They're smart and they're articulate about the construction business."

Said John Wood, Mortenson's principal in charge of the ballpark project, "We've never worked with a classier group of people than the Twins. Their handshake is as good as a contract. That's been the highlight of this experience."

M. A. "Mort" Mortenson

Walt Disney Concert Hall in Los Angeles was built by Mortenson Construction in 2003.

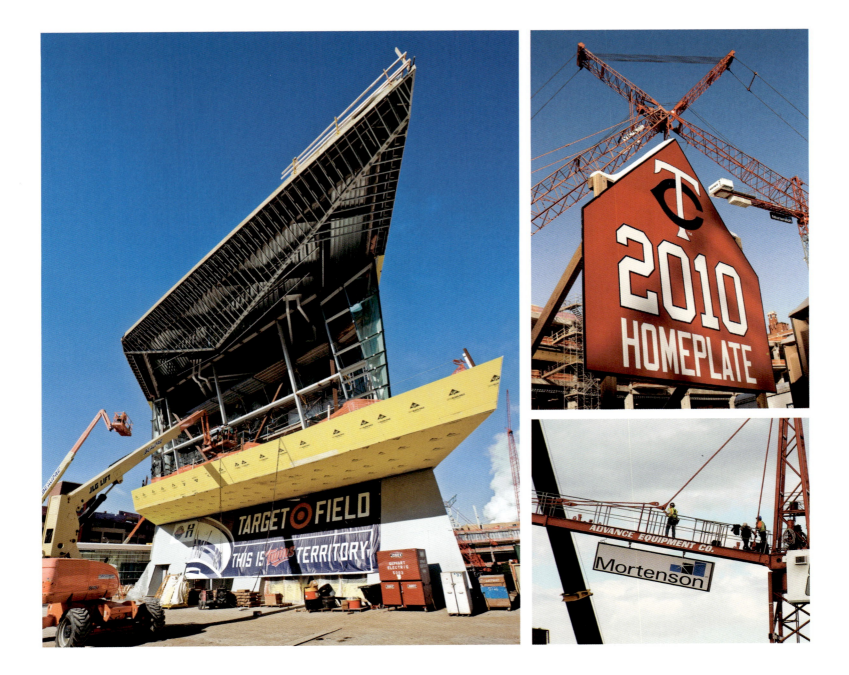

Despite advanced technology,

Mortenson's projects are still driven by

face-to-face **human** contacts.

Do you wish to rise?

Begin by **descending**.

You plan a tower that will

pierce the clouds?

Lay first the foundation

of **humility**.

—*Saint Augustine*

DIG IN THE DIRT BEFORE BUILDING TO THE SKY

As Saint Augustine suggested in the fifth century, any construction project, whether spiritual or temporal, begins by digging in the dirt. Investigating the soil conditions beneath the ballpark area was the first step of construction.

Mortenson's engineers already knew quite a lot about the district's geology before excavations began in the spring of 2007 because of the company's work more than 20 years earlier on Target Center, the Timberwolves basketball arena located just to the east of the site. Half of Target Center, along with most of downtown Minneapolis, rests on a firm sandstone ledge, but workers had to fortify the western half of the building with 40-foot pilings because the rock formation falls so sharply. Two blocks to the west, at the site of the

Groundbreaking ceremony, August 30, 2007

Setting the pilings, September 2007

ballpark, bedrock lies nearly 100 feet below the surface, forming an ancient riverbed deeper and wider than the Mississippi. The notion of a ballpark "floating" on a spongy layer of sediment was an obvious impossibility.

To provide a firm foundation, engineers devised a system of 3,396 pilings made of 10-inch steel pipe, driven 95 feet to bedrock, and filled with concrete. Laid end to end, the pilings would cover just over 62 miles. That's an astounding amount of steel to sink into the ground to support a project the size of a ballpark. The underground portion of the project took extraordinary time and effort for other reasons as well, namely major complications along its western edge.

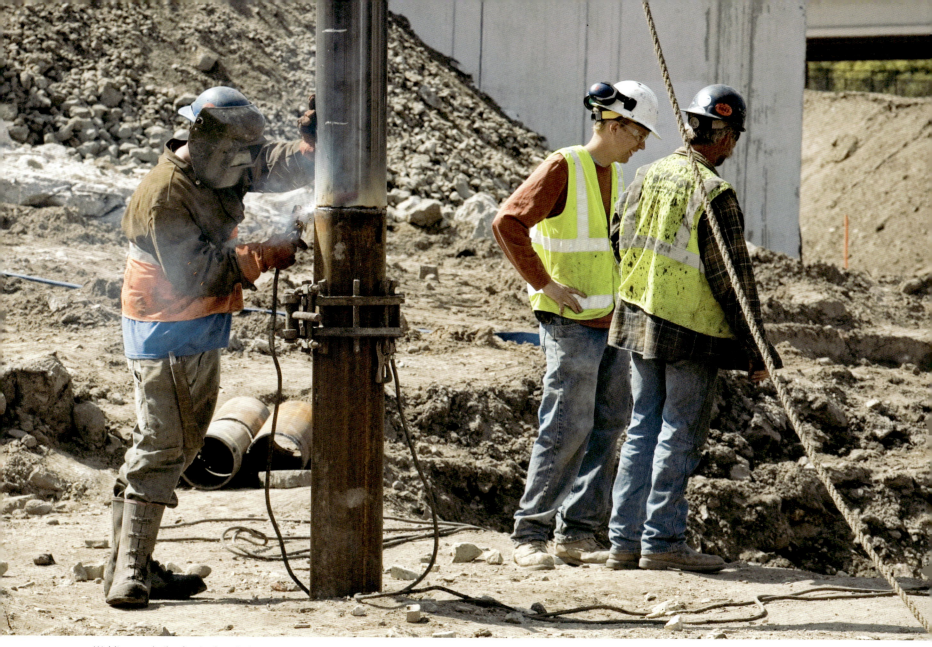

Welding steel piles for the foundation system

One problem involved a branch of Bassett Creek. The creek, enclosed in a double-box culvert 15 feet below the surface, ran where pilings for the third-base grandstand needed to go. Workers could not disturb the waterway, so a subterranean roof of sorts had to be built over the top. The roof was made of transfer beams: 52 reinforced concrete girders of various sizes that, in effect, divided and redistributed the load from the stadium's columns to each side of the 22-foot-wide culvert and tied them to the pilings. It was a significant undertaking. A few of the beams were nearly 8 feet thick and weighed 400 tons. Because the surrounding soil was so soft, elaborate barricades had to be constructed to keep dirt from sloughing into the work zones.

Indeed, the condition of the soil posed a special problem. Eight "hot spots" with excessive levels of mercury were discovered and sent to a special landfill. Much of the rest of the soil, although not seriously contaminated, was considered unsuitable. More than 160,000 tons of soil was scooped up and transported to landfills, at a cost of more than $2.5 million.

Left: Filling the transfer beams with concrete

CERTIFIED GREEN

TARGET FIELD IS AMONG THE MOST ENVIRONMENTALLY CONSCIOUS SPORTS VENUES IN THE WORLD. On April 8, 2010, the U.S. Green Building Council (USGBC) awarded the ballpark Leadership in Energy and Environmental Design (LEED) Silver Certification, making Target Field only the second major league ballpark to achieve that status. (The Washington Nationals' park was the first, achieving LEED certification in 2008.) Target Field collected the most certification points ever awarded to a ballpark—beating out Nationals Park by two points—to make it the greenest ballpark in the nation. From the start, the Twins' new home was designed to save energy, minimize environmental impact, and remain a sustainable neighbor long into the future.

Following are some of Target Field's environmental benefits:

- It replaced a large surface parking lot that posed a storm-water-runoff threat to the Mississippi River.
- It sits adjacent to the Twin Cities' primary rail-transit hub, thus minimizing the need for fans to drive to games.
- It is located only a few blocks from Minneapolis' downtown core, giving more than 200,000 office workers, residents, and daily visitors a short walk or train ride to the games.
- It is located on the Cedar Lake Trail, a popular bike route.

In addition, the stadium's downtown location should make it a catalyst for urban revitalization, encouraging the kind of mixed-use neighborhoods that help reduce traffic congestion and cut energy use.

That the ballpark sits next to the Hennepin Energy Recovery Center (HERC) doesn't hurt its green profile either. HERC is an innovative complex that converts about 365,000 tons of solid waste per year to electricity. Recycled steam from HERC is used to heat the playing field and the ballpark's domestic water supply.

Indeed, conserving water is a major function of Target Field's design. Water-conserving plumbing fixtures save an estimated 4.2 million gallons of water per year and reduce overall water use by 30 percent. In a groundbreaking partnership between the Twins and Minneapolis-based Pentair Inc., a global firm that specializes in water technology, the natural turf at Target Field is watered with recycled rainwater that is processed and purified onsite. The half-million-dollar custom recycling system sets a new standard for sports stadiums worldwide.

Rainwater from the ballpark's seven-acre main seating bowl and playing field percolates through an underground drainage system and collects in a huge 100,000-gallon cistern buried beneath the outfield warning track. The water is filtered, disinfected with ultraviolet light, filtered again,

> "We are absolutely thrilled about the **LEED Silver Certification** for the ballpark.
>
> The [Minnesota Ballpark Authority] is pleased that our investment will pay dividends
>
> for years to come as fans learn more about the importance
>
> of sustainable design when they visit Target Field."
>
> —*Steve Cramer, chair of the Minnesota Ballpark Authority*

and pumped into a 5,000-gallon holding tank located near the bullpens in left field. The ultra-clean water is then reused to irrigate the field and wash down the lower level seating area.

The recycling saves the city of Minneapolis more than 2 million gallons of water annually, or about half of what the ballpark needs. Only about 5 percent of the recycled water becomes "backwash" discharged into the city's sanitary sewers.

Other green features incorporated into Target Field include the following:

- Energy-conserving exterior lights produce less glare and realize a 35 percent energy savings over conventional field lighting.
- Building materials used in the ballpark, including concrete, steel, tile, and floor coverings, contain a minimum of 10 percent recycled content.
- Carpet glues, paints, and adhesives have low VOC (volatile organic compound) contents.
- Wood used in the building comes from forests certified by the Forest Service Council as practicing sound conservation and management methods.
- About 25 percent of the building materials, by cost, were produced within 500 miles of the Twin Cities, thus cutting transportation costs and promoting the regional economy.
- Much of the landscaping is nourished by reused water, thus avoiding excessive irrigation.

During the construction process, some 70 percent of the construction waste was recycled or reused, thus reducing trips to landfills. In addition, interior rooms and ventilation systems were sealed off to minimize dust accumulation.

"Stadiums are iconic buildings," said Mark Andrew of GreenMark, the Minneapolis-based green marketing firm that specializes in sports projects. "For a stadium to go green has a big impact in the community and nationwide."

Andrew first contacted the Twins about pursuing a green venture in 2001, and he later produced a 200-page memo on the long-term advantages of green design and operation. Jim Pohlad's enthusiasm about a ballpark that would be compatible with the environment was the crucial point, Andrew said. "The Twins are very committed, and they deserve a lot of credit."

Upon receiving the Silver Certification from the USGBC in April 2010, Pohlad spoke of the significance of the historic moment. "Gaining LEED certification has been a longstanding goal for the Twins, Hennepin County, and the Minnesota Ballpark Authority as we have collectively shared the responsibility to ensure strong environmental stewardship," said Pohlad. "It's our sincere hope that the sustainability aspects of Target Field will provide inspiration to other local, regional, and national projects of this magnitude."

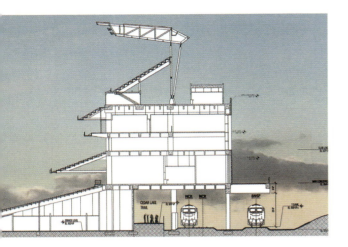

In the end,

a **cooperative spirit**

prevailed.

BALLPARKS AND FREIGHT TRAINS

An even bigger construction obstacle than the creek and the soil quality was the freight railroad line running through the west side of the site. The double-track line is a branch of the BNSF Railway's Northern Transcon, a busy 2,200-mile cargo corridor running from Seattle to Chicago. Although the branch line carries only 7 to 14 trains per day, the railroad insisted that its schedule not be disrupted.

"Some of the early negotiations were so tough that we thought we'd lost the project," said Bruce Miller, the architect from Kansas City–based Populous who oversaw the daily design work. In the end, a cooperative spirit prevailed, he said, because none of the partners, including the railroad, wanted to be seen as the villain who cost Minnesota a ballpark.

Early drawings showed freight trains running directly beneath the stands along the third-base side, but for various reasons, including liability, the main track was shifted 63 feet to the west so that freight trains would run beneath the stadium's promenade and not beneath the stadium itself. Two sidings, however, one for Northstar commuter trains, do run beneath the third-base stands. The 20-foot-wide Cedar Lake Trail, a popular bicycle route, runs through the same tunnel.

Building the ballpark beside and over the BNSF tracks while not disrupting train service was a nightmare for Mortenson's construction schedule. Often, the contractor didn't know from one day to the next how many trains would be coming through and when. For a year and a half, the ballpark project had to post flagmen along the tracks to warn construction crews that trains were approaching. Cranes, trucks, and other equipment then had to be quickly disengaged and moved away as trains passed.

Working over and under active highways posed further complications. The ballpark's right-field structure rests on three bridges that had to be built over the top of Interstate 394. As a result, freeway traffic passes directly beneath the right-field seats, the ticket office, the team store, the Metropolitan Club, and Target Plaza, which serves as the ballpark's main entrance. Keeping the freeway and its ramps open during construction was no small challenge. The project turned the roadway into a three-block tunnel requiring new lighting and ventilation.

Meanwhile, on the project's south side, the Seventh Street Bridge, a main traffic conduit between the downtown core and Olson Memorial Highway, had to remain open while a loading dock and steam pipes were constructed beneath it.

To the north, the Fifth Street Bridge had to be reconfigured and fortified to carry both autos and light-rail trains, and the bridge itself had to serve as a light-rail station. A storage building had to be constructed beneath the bridge, and an escalator building had to be squeezed into the ballpark's left-field corner to provide light-rail passengers a way to connect to the Northstar commuter trains running below. As if that wasn't enough, a new sewer had to be constructed below that.

Taken all together, these complex, multi-level projects required extraordinary cooperation among city, county, metro, state, and federal agencies and a number of private businesses, each with its own rules, procedures, and rivalries. "It came very much down to good human relationships to make this happen," said Mehls. "Just getting the project out of the ground was a big accomplishment."

Random sensations

are coming together

in a **complete**

composition.

CONSTRUCTION AS SYMPHONY

Ever been to the symphony? For a novice, it can be a bewildering experience. Violins saw away at the melody while cellos and violas try to harmonize. Woodwinds and brass seem off on separate adventures while the percussion section pounds away aimlessly, or so it seems. But as you follow the conductor's baton, and as you allow the whole of the music to penetrate your defenses, it all begins to make sense. Everyone is, in fact, playing in concert. Random sensations are coming together in a complete composition. And you walk away awestruck by the skill of the musicians, the talent of the conductor to manage these various players, and the genius of the composer to have imagined it all before setting it down on paper.

Construction is like that.

On a typical day during the building of Target Field, more than 800 men and women swarmed over the site performing hundreds of separate tasks simultaneously. Hard hats bobbed up and down. Yellow vests darted here and there as workers carried lunch coolers, drove forklifts, and gathered together to study problems. Stacks of pipes, rebar, and drywall stood at the ready. Sparks from welders' torches broke out sporadically. And the noise? Well, there was grinding, drilling, sawing, hammering, the roar of motors of every type, and the relentless *beep, beep, beep* of a dozen vehicles backing up at once.

SEEING THE LETTERS HOISTED TO THE TOP OF THE SCOREBOARD WAS A THRILL for many stadium workers, neighbors, and commuters along Interstate 394. The giant Twins logo was a reminder that this was no ordinary construction project but a place where baseball would soon be played. The five letters and swoosh were raised on May 26 to 28, 2009, offering a sneak preview of the team's new lettering style—a subtle departure from the font used since 1987.

The red letters, which are made of aluminum and plastic, were fabricated by Architectural Graphics of Virginia Beach and shipped to Minneapolis by truck. The sign was hoisted in seven sections beginning with the swoosh. High winds played havoc with the "w," delaying installation for a day. The entire logo stands 26 feet tall, 49 feet wide, and 1 foot thick, and it weighs nearly 8,250 pounds. Low-voltage LED lights were attached in June, making the sign a baseball beacon seen for miles.

KEITH HERZOG

Crane operator
Sauk Rapids, Minnesota

Crane operators are the fighter pilots of construction. They "fly" the biggest machines and deliver the biggest payloads. Their hands are steady and experienced enough to guide monster beams up into the sky while calculating the wind's direction and velocity so that the steel doesn't begin to "helicopter" in a way that imperils the ironworkers stationed to pluck it out of the air and settle it into place.

"I need to make sure that those guys go home with ten fingers and toes and the same body parts at the end of the day that they came in with," said Keith Herzog, the crane operator from Shakopee-based DCCI who set much of the iron at Target Field. Herzog's cockpit monitors give him readings on the weight of his load, the reach of the crane's boom, and the speed and direction of the wind, among other conditions. "Mentally, you've got to be prepared for the job and always be thinking ahead about where the iron needs to go and how to get it there the right way," he said.

Herzog, operating a 275-ton-capacity Manitowoc crawler crane, set the last piece of structural steel on June 5, 2009. "It was a baby, only 5,800 pounds," he said, but it had to travel 167 feet into a wind blowing from the northwest at 20 miles an hour. Hoisting the beam—which was signed by hundreds of his fellow workers—and setting it high over the left-field corner was a milestone for the project and for Herzog.

"Cranes are in my blood," he said, explaining that his dad, also a crane man, introduced him to the job when he was a kid on the Iron Range. For more than three decades, his career has taken him to construction sites all across the country. But his favorite jobs are close to home.

Installing the hardwood mural of Kirby Puckett on the Club Level required care and craftsmanship.

Daily stretching was an integral part of keeping workers safe and alert during the long days on the job.

A project the size of a ballpark needed tower cranes and crawler cranes, power shovels and all-terrain forklifts. It needed people and equipment to dig big holes and to drive piles with that terrible relentless banging. It needed crane operators to fight the wind to land 12-ton crossbeams on a dime 100 feet in the air. It needed truck drivers to deliver components and concrete workers to pump the slushy mix to the far corners of the site. It needed precision millworkers, sheet-metal artisans, drywallers, quarry workers, welders, stonecutters, plumbers, electricians, pipefitters, painters, masons, ironworkers, caulkers, and concrete finishers. It needed computer geeks and accountants, field architects and foremen, engineers and project managers.

Most of all, it needed a general superintendent who, like an orchestra conductor, sees the big picture, understands every job, knows exactly when each job needs to be done and how each task affects every other task. A good general superintendent is a perfectionist with an eye for detail and a swagger in his step. He's a tough guy, willing to crack the whip but able also to inspire workers, earn their respect, and compel them to work as a team. On the Target Field project, that guy was Dave Mansell.

A variety of cranes, crawler cranes, power shovels, and other heavy equipment busy at work on Target Field

"Mentally, you've got to be **prepared** for the job

and always be thinking ahead about where the iron

needs to go and how to get it there the right way."

—Keith Herzog, crane operator

"Working on this project has been very **special**."

—*Debbie Gilmore, electrician*

DEBBIE GILMORE

Electrician
Oak Grove, Minnesota

In 1992 Debbie Gilmore traded in her office job for a hard hat and work boots, and she hasn't looked back. "I got tired of working 80 hours for 40 hours' pay," she said. Now, as an electrician for St. Paul–based Gephart Electric, Gilmore gets more variety—and a lot more exercise. "I walk 10 miles a day on this project, and I'm not exaggerating," she said on a spring day in 2009, working high on the terrace level at Target Field. "And I can tell you it's 190 steps to get up here from the service level down at the bottom."

As a baseball fan, working on the ballpark was a thrilling experience for Gilmore. "I'm a Nordeast girl," she said, talking about growing up in Northeast Minneapolis and following the Twins. "Working on this project has been very special." A lot of people don't understand the massive amount of electrical circuitry that goes into a ballpark, she said, listing everything from lights to scoreboards to sound systems and concession areas.

Gilmore was impressed by the complexity of the job, the care and quality of the work, and the emphasis on safety. "This is a very busy place. There's precast [concrete] flying overhead, and you've got to be aware of what's happening around you all the time."

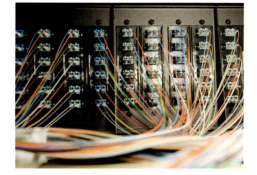

A DAY WITH THE CONSTRUCTION BOSS

DAVE MANSELL, A LARGER-THAN-LIFE FIXTURE AT MORTENSON, filled the role of general superintendent on the ballpark project. He dominates a room. He is loud, profane, brilliant, funny, caring, and relentless in moving a job forward.

"Dave is the smartest guy I've ever known in construction," said Scott Keller, a millworker with J. R. Jones Fixture Company of Minneapolis. "He's tough, he's honest, and when he calls my phone I pick it up. Whenever Dave calls with a job to do, I'll be there."

Mansell inspires that kind of loyalty. Every big construction project has its own personality. Target Field has Dave Mansell's personality hardwired into every nook and cranny. As much as any ballplayer, team owner, politician, or designer, Target Field is his ballpark.

Mansell's ride up the construction ladder wasn't easy. He failed to finish high school, then lost his license as a truck driver because of speeding violations. But something clicked when he started as a laborer around a construction site. He wanted to know not only his job but everyone else's, and how they all fit together. He was fascinated by every detail and couldn't stop trying to learn everything. "If I didn't understand something, I'd have to figure it out," he said. "I've always had a good memory."

Over time he used his phenomenal memory to build a multidimensional matrix in his head about construction—a kind of mental map of space and time. He has the unusual talent of being able to imagine a finished project in all its complexity, then work backward to determine which piece needs to go first, second, and so on, and how one piece impacts all the others. "It's like you have this tub with a million Legos," he said, "but you have to fit them all together in the right order and in a certain period of time."

Mansell strung together a 21-year career at Mortenson, working projects in 13 states before landing the Target Field assignment. "Without a doubt we have the best craft workers in the country right here in Minneapolis," he said, scanning the project on a perfect spring day in 2009.

More than two years earlier he had written an intricate construction schedule composed of more than 14,000 activities. As the project proceeded, he checked them off one by one.

"Dave is the embodiment of the schedule," said George Fantauzza, a field architect with Populous and one of a dozen or so architects and other designers who worked onsite to coordinate daily tasks with contractors. Fantauzza's point was an important one: The complex, step-by-step computerized schedule with 14,000 coordinated activities needed to express itself in human form, face to face, with 800 workers. That human form was Mansell.

During one typical morning on the job, which began after a 45-minute drive from his home in Roberts, Wisconsin, Mansell met with more than 100 supervisors in a construction trailer at 6:15 in the morning to preview specific tasks for the coming weeks. "We got to get all our [stuff] off the field by the end of the month," he said, referring to the two dozen pieces of heavy equipment working to erect the final bits of basic structure. "There's a whole bunch of grass growing down in Colorado, and it can't wait to get up here," he said, alluding to the stadium turf waiting to be installed.

He groused about delays in the arrival of ipe, a Brazilian hardwood that covers a portion of the ballpark exterior. "It's stuck in the mud somewhere in the rainforest. I might have to go down there and get it myself," he said.

Mansell mentioned a large etching of Kirby Puckett going up in one of the clubs. "Whatever you do, don't dent Kirby's forehead," he instructed. And he ordered foremen to enforce cleanliness on the work site, saying, "We don't need no chicken bones in the seats."

STAYING SAFE ON A DANGEROUS JOB

MORTENSON IS OBSESSED WITH SAFETY. Making sure that every one of the 800 or so workers returned home each evening with all limbs intact was priority number one on the Target Field job.

First thing every morning, the entire construction crew gathered for 10 minutes of stretching exercises. It is a daily ritual on Mortenson projects, aimed at promoting the physical dexterity and alertness needed to avoid injury, as well as building camaraderie among the workers.

As the general superintendent overseeing the ballpark project, Dave Mansell wasn't shy about letting workers know when he caught them cutting corners. On one particular morning, he chewed out a crew of workers for taking an unauthorized short-cut across a section of right-field bleachers. He reprimanded an electrician for installing a light fixture while standing precariously on the edge of a counter. Near the Twins' dugout, Mansell instructed a mason on the art of lifting stones in a way that won't cause back injury.

"They don't want to see me coming," he said. "They think I'm the evil troll."

Then he ducked into a meeting of new workers, telling them, "One time I found a guy standing wrong on a ladder, and he sees me watching him. He comes down, looks me in the eye, and says, 'I'm sorry, Dave.' And I tell him, 'Don't tell me you're sorry. Go home and tell your wife and kids you're sorry. What's going to happen when you fall down 20 feet and crack your head open? Who's gonna be sorry then?'"

"What it boils down to is instilling the right attitude, and I'm the one who has to convey it," Mansell said.

Mansell acknowledged the conflicts embedded in his job. He must bring the project in on time and on budget. He must ensure that the work is of the highest quality. But he must avoid cutting corners on safety to meet those objectives. "The most important thing is that people get back home every night to enjoy their families," he said. He includes himself in that dictum. He and his wife, Kelly, who also works for Mortenson, have two young daughters.

CONSTRUCTING BY COMPUTER

As is common with any major construction undertaking, the design team from Populous and the construction team from Mortenson encountered problems relating to the site and the scope of the work. Some were challenges they anticipated going in; others were surprises that arose as the project proceeded.

Many of these problems were best sorted out by using advanced computer modeling. Mortenson's remarkable Building Information Model (BIM) provided detailed illustrations in three dimensions from any angle of any feature in the ballpark. If an air-conditioning duct ran where a water pipe needed to go, the model could spot the conflict and help builders resolve it.

The computer model also showed the entire project in a fourth dimension: time. The ballpark, in all its detail, could be run as a kind of movie as it went up piece by piece. That made B.I.M. essential to plotting the project's "fast track" scheduling, a process by which construction began on some parts of the building before detailed drawings were finished. Indeed, drawing and constructing proceeded simultaneously for about a year, a process that required close monitoring by designers and builders.

"There's no **I**

in a job like this."

—*Marcus Scott, sheet metal worker*

WORKER PROFILE
MARCUS SCOTT
Sheet metal worker
Brooklyn Park, Minnesota

On a bright spring day in 2009, Marcus Scott was deep in the innards of Target Field installing heating and air-conditioning ducts. "I've been on a lot of small mom-and-pop projects where they cut corners, but not here. This is going to be nice! They've given us the flexibility to do things the right way. We're all pros, so it's really nice when you see a job that's devoted to quality and not just to getting by," he said.

Scott, who grew up in St. Paul's Frogtown neighborhood, reflected on what it's like to work on a big project during hard economic times, when so many others in the construction trades are without jobs.

"I don't feel lucky, that's not really it," he said. "When so many of your brothers and sisters are hurting, it's no time to think about me, me, me. There's no 'I' in a job like this. The right way to think about this is, Well, it's my turn now. Maybe I'll be laid off next time, so I've got to be ready. You've got to keep your mind strong."

Scott, who works for Metropolitan Mechanical Contractors Inc., based in Eden Prairie, praised the Target Field job site and the professionalism of the contractors involved. "They understand that a happy worker is a good worker," he said.

The unusually long design-build overlap was needed to accommodate the project's snug fit and Minnesota's severe climate. Limited space outside the project's footprint required the ballpark to be built from the inside out, meaning that cranes and other big pieces of equipment had to be stationed on the ballpark's field. But, to establish grass in Minnesota's climate, sod had to be laid six months before the ballpark's opening, which, in turn, meant that all heavy equipment had to be removed from the field by mid- to late summer 2009. As a result, all major structural work had to be completed long before the ballpark's scheduled opening in spring of 2010.

All of that phasing and staging of design and construction required extraordinary coordination among architects, construction crews, and the computer model. Indeed, the entire project unfolded in an atypical way.

Normal ballpark construction starts at home plate and proceeds down each foul line simultaneously, with competition breaking out between first-base and third-base crews. But with workers still dealing with the underground waterway and the railroad problems along the third-base line, construction at Target Field had to begin in the right-field corner and move clockwise. The idea was to keep digging along the third-base line while the first-base line structure went up and was finished off before moving toward the third-base side.

Building the structure in complete phased sections, rather than deck by deck all the way around, meant that a wider variety of building materials had to be delivered on a "just in time" basis. Limited space to store materials made the delivery schedule even more critical.

Altogether, Target Field is composed of eight distinct buildings separated by expansion joints, which are three-inch gaps that allow for the expansion and contraction of the structure as temperatures change. Many of the ballpark's outdoor spaces are located directly above finished indoor areas, so special care was taken to build sub roofs and interior drainage systems to prevent moisture from seeping in.

Unlike other sporting venues, where sections of stands repeat themselves, there's almost no redundancy in a traditional baseball layout like Target Field's. Every section is, in effect, custom built, which makes the project vastly more difficult and more costly. It's the main reason why a ballpark, on a square-foot basis, costs twice as much as a football stadium or a basketball/hockey arena.

All of these intricate time, space, and cost relationships were driven by B.I.M. "It's hard to see how we could have built this so quickly without the model," said Miller.

Because the project and the site were so compact, the ballpark had to be built from the inside out, with construction equipment stationed on the field rather than on the periphery.

Construction on the first-base side was completed much earlier than the third-base side.

Crews installed Target Field's scoreboard in early May 2009. The massive structure measures 101 feet wide by 57 feet high and weighs a total 47,500 pounds. The components were manufactured in Redwood Falls, Minnesota, and Brookings, South Dakota, by Daktronics Inc. It took six days to lift the board's 72 sections into place, connect them, and attach them to the steel framework.

WORKER PROFILE
DARRELL CHAMBERS
Caulker
Minneapolis, Minnesota

On a sunny morning in May 2009, Darrell Chambers was putting the finishing touches on sealing the spaces between the beautiful stones that cover the porch cantilevering slightly out over the right-field wall.

"Finally we're going to have a respectable ballpark," said Chambers, who spent years living in the Bay Area and watching baseball in Oakland and at San Francisco's new waterfront ballpark. The former Marine is back home living in Minneapolis' Uptown district. "I couldn't figure out how they were going to fit this ballpark in here, but it's going to be magic," he said. "There's not . . . a bad seat in the house."

Chambers, who works for Eden Prairie–based Seal-Treat Inc., said it's especially nice to be working on a high-profile project. "Everybody's looking at this thing, so you can't make a mistake. There's a big push on quality," he said, adding that the site required more than 18 miles of sealing work. There are a lot of ways that water can damage an outdoor ballpark, he said, if it's not carefully waterproofed.

"I couldn't figure out how they were going to fit this ballpark in here, but it's going to be **magic**."

—*Darrell Chambers, caulker*

MANKATO LIMESTONE Bringing a Distinctive "Minnesota Look"

IT'S ONLY NATURAL TO THINK OF TARGET FIELD AS BEING ALL NEW, but its stunning limestone exterior is actually 450 million years old. That puts much of the ballpark squarely in the Ordovician Period of the Second Paleozoic Era—or about 2.5 million centuries before dinosaurs and 4.5 million centuries before Babe Ruth.

The limestone was formed from sediment at the bottom of an ancient sea. It hardened and thickened at a rate of one inch every 2,500 years until about 10,000 years ago when glacial movements exposed the stone to the earth's surface. Humans, when they finally arrived on the scene, admired the stone's beauty and eventually put it to use. By the 1860s, settlers around Mankato began carving up the outcroppings for foundations, bridges, and other structures. When concrete began to dominate the construction business in the early 1900s, most of the quarries went bust. But a local stonecutter named Paul J. Vetter began buying up the rocky ravines near the village of Kasota, north of Mankato, in the 1930s. In 1954 he and his sons opened their own business, just in time to catch the postwar building boom.

The Vetter Stone Company has since become a Minnesota institution. Its high-grade dolomitic limestone—often called Kasota stone—lies generally between 6 and 16 feet below the surface. The layers are remarkably thick for limestone (between 4 and 7 feet), and the colors vary from the rustic golden tans used on Target Field to shades of buff, gray, and pink. The Vetters estimate that there's enough rock on their property to keep the business going for another 500 years. The great thickness of the Kasota layers, their color variation, and their easy access from the surface make the Mankato stone deposits among the world's most valuable.

"There's a lot of limestone in the world, but high-quality limestone is more rare than granite or marble," said Howard Vetter, the company's chairman and a cog in the family business for more than a half-century.

The company has a worldwide reputation. Vetter limestone dresses U.S. embassies in Moscow and Abu Dhabi, the Japanese National Museum in Osaka, corporate headquarters for Nippon Telephone and Telegraph in Tokyo and Samsung in Seoul, the Smithsonian's National Museum of the American Indian in Washington, D.C., and PNC Park, the Pittsburgh Pirates' ballpark, to name a few examples.

Among the many local buildings clad in Vetter stone are the Wells Fargo Tower and the WCCO television building in downtown Minneapolis, each showing off the sandy-gold shades that have become something of a Minnesota signature.

Both Howard and his son, Ron, the company president, speak with reverence about the timelessness of their product. Howard's office contains a stone wall with imprints of ancient sea lilies. Both men wonder aloud about the cataclysmic events that must have determined the changes in color and texture over the eons.

Ron says that the stone's primordial and perpetual nature appeals to people, as do its color and texture. "There's a warmth that draws people in," he says. "People tend to want to touch it."

The Vetters were so excited about the possibility that their stone would clad the Twins ballpark that they began stockpiling large pieces eight months before a final decision was made. In all, about 2,400 tons of stone—about 100 truckloads—were selected for Target Field. Most of the stone was sawed into thin slices in the Vetters' Mankato plant, then shipped to Gage Brothers, a concrete specialist in Sioux Falls, South Dakota, where the stone slices were fit into large concrete panels for the ballpark's exterior. Each panel had its own drawing. The measurements were so precise that only three stones had to be resized. The exterior stones were arranged for a mix of colors and textures, with a greater number of darker stones placed at the stadium's base to form a visual anchor. Other stones were hand cut at the stadium site for more detailed work. The Twins wanted—and paid extra—to bring as much stone as possible to the ballpark's interior. It is featured, for example, on the cantilevered right-field porch, on facings above the dugouts, and on the infield wall at ground level.

Overall, the stone on the ballpark is meant to emulate Minnesota's river bluffs with their layers of golden rock formations. "We've done a lot of jobs around the world, but as Minnesotans, this one is very personal for us," said Ron Vetter. "It's very special."

"We feel **privileged** to be a part of this project.

The Twins are an important part of what it means to be a Minnesotan."

—*Ron Vetter, president, Vetter Stone Company*

Jerry Bell, president of Twins Sports Inc., views the Vetter Stone quarry near Mankato in November 2007.

Raw limestone blocks marked for Target Field

Limestone for the ballpark's exterior was delivered by the truckloads during 2008.

Caulking the limestone exterior

The stunning limestone exterior is actually **450 million years old**.

That puts much of the ballpark squarely in the Ordovician Period

of the Second Paleozoic Era—or about 2.5 million centuries

before dinosaurs and 4.5 million centuries before Babe Ruth.

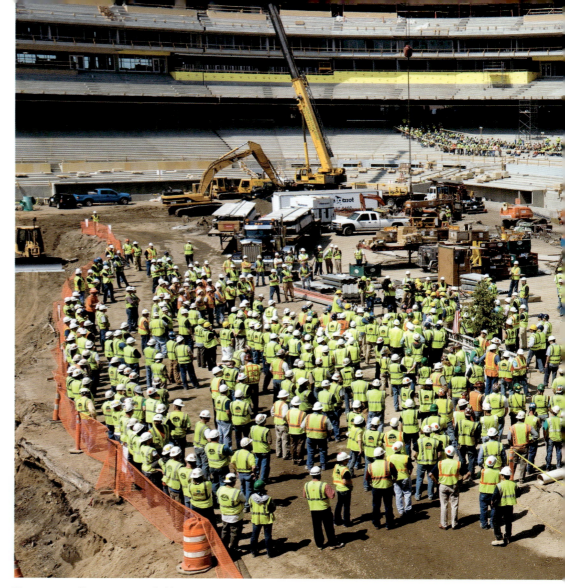

The topping-off ceremony was held on June 5, 2009, as the last beam at Target Field was put into place.

FINISHING TOUCHES

In the end, more than 3,300 craft workers helped to build Target Field. Thousands more worked offsite to cut stones, assemble signs and seats, pour pre-cast concrete sections, and perform hundreds of other tasks. More than a quarter of the onsite workers were minorities, and six percent were women. Nearly one-third of the construction contracts went to small firms, or those owned by minorities or women.

More than 90 percent of the workers were from the Twin Cities metro region. The "Twins" letters on the scoreboard were fabricated in Virginia, the seats came from Michigan, a shipment of reclaimed hardwood came from Brazil, and some tile was shipped in from Italy. Still, according to Mortenson estimates, more than 90 percent of the dollar value of the ballpark's construction—including labor, supervision, materials, fees, and equipment— came from Minnesota contractors or those just across the border in Wisconsin and South Dakota.

It took about one thousand days and two million worker hours to build the one-million-square-foot structure. Some 110 subcontractors were hired as partners in the monumental project, more than four-fifths of them from Minnesota.

It took about

one thousand days and

two million worker hours

to build the one-million-

square-foot structure.

TARGET FIELD: *A Local Project*

Total number of craft workers on the Target Field project	3,300
Percentage of craft workers from the **Twin Cities metro area**	90
Percentage of subcontractors **headquartered in Minnesota**	82
Percentage of dollar value of **building materials produced locally**	25

HOW TO BUILD A BALLPARK

HOW EXACTLY BUILDINGS GET BUILT IS A MYSTERY to almost everyone. David Macaulay, author of *The Way Things Work* and other illustrated works, is the world's best-known demystifyer of the construction process. Macaulay once said that the key to understanding is to ask question upon question until "this thing, this structure, this dam, this skyscraper . . . begins to take shape and you begin to understand why it looks the way it does."

Once Target Field got out of the ground, it began rather quickly to look the way it does today. It rose much like any other five-story building.

🌿 First, the tops of the underground pilings were sealed with "pile caps," large concrete slabs with formations of steel rods (rebar) inside. Some of the rebar was connected to the pilings below and some protruded from the top to form the base for columns that would be poured above.

🌿 Vertical columns were then assembled in a similar way. The process is called "cast in place." Giant molds, or forms, made of steel and plywood and filled with rebar were hoisted into the correct positions. Concrete was then pumped into the forms through long hoses from the mixing trucks. After the concrete hardened, the forms were removed, revealing the columns.

Horizontal concrete decks were then assembled by a similar process and attached to the columns to form the basic skeleton of the building. Target Field has five such decks. The service level, located at the same elevation as the field, houses maintenance spaces and team clubhouses. The second deck forms the main concourse that overlooks the primary seating bowl. The third and fourth decks house clubs and suites for premium ticket holders. The fifth deck supports general seating near the top of the structure.

Rakers, the diagonal pieces that slant down toward the field, were then attached to the decks. The lower-deck rakers were made of steel-reinforced concrete that had been "precast" off site, transported to the construction zone, and lifted into place by cranes. Rakers hung from the three upper decks were made of steel beams. Precast concrete stadia were then attached to the rakers. These are the big stair-stepped sections on which seats are later fastened.

One of the most dramatic construction feats was performed by giant crawler cranes, which were stationed on the field because of a lack of room outside the stadium. The crane operators lifted huge concrete panels wrapped in beautiful sandy-colored stone up and over the top of the stands, then, "flying blind," lowered the panels into their places on the structure's exterior, forming the outside walls of the ballpark. It was, as the contractors called it, building "from the inside out."

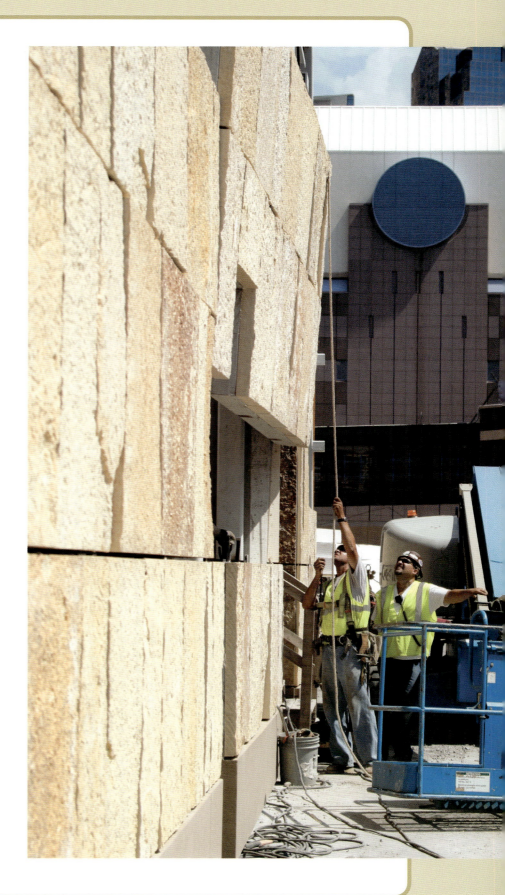

The last segment set in place was the sleek steel canopy at the top of the ballpark. Its angular sections had to be hoisted by cranes 150 feet over the playing field. "The canopy has the most complicated steel geometry of the entire project," according to Mortenson's Eric Keleny, "partly because of the lights." Unlike other ballparks, no light poles were included at Target Field. Instead, lights were fit directly into the canopy structure and embedded in the scoreboard, giving the ballpark a streamlined look found nowhere else in sports, and keeping a relatively low profile in scale with the surrounding neighborhood.

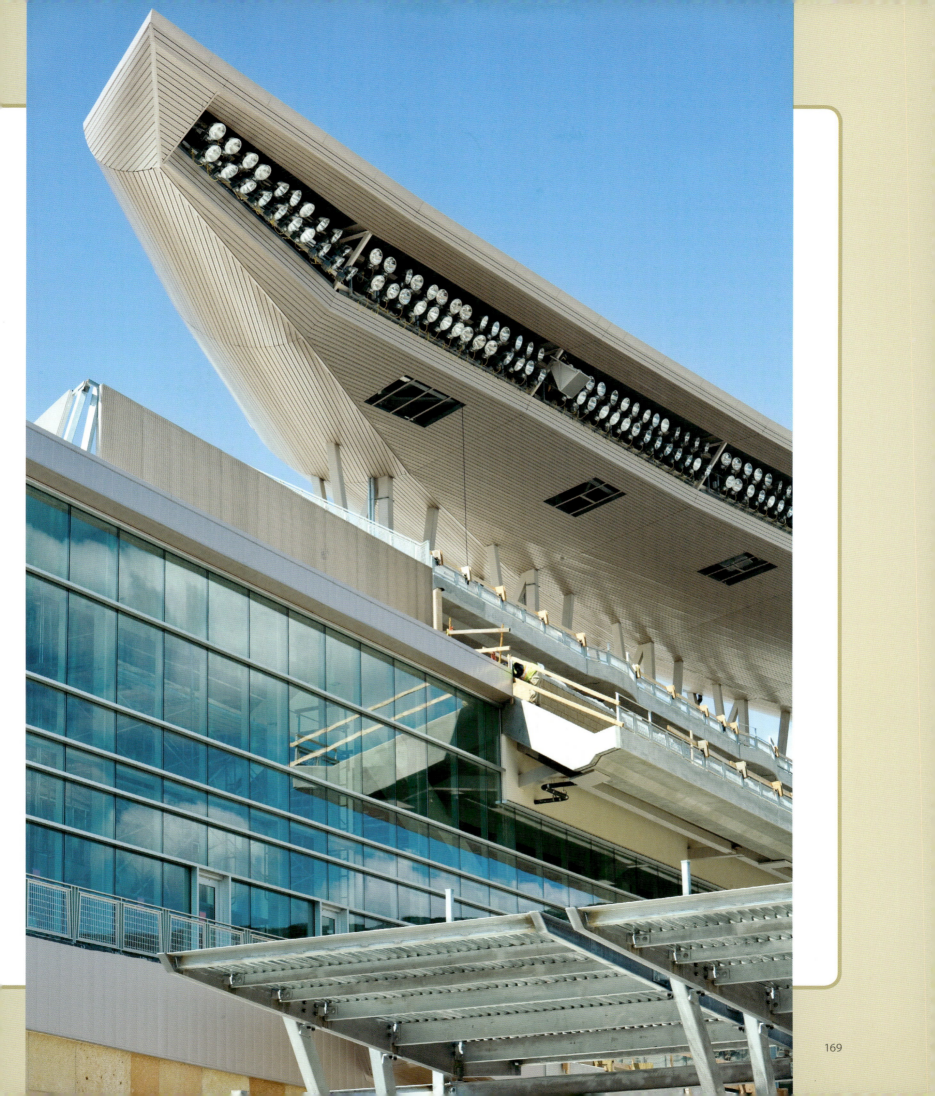

THE GREEN GRASS OF HOME

On a perfect summer night in 2009, under clear skies, with a temperature of 75 degrees and a slight breeze blowing, with downtown lights twinkling and expectations running high, the first truckload of sod arrived at Target Field.

Immediately, the first roll was pulled off the truck and escorted onto the barren field by a platoon of helmeted workmen who began to tamp and tend as the sod was unfurled along the left-field line. Photographers and dignitaries leaned forward, almost reverently. Spectators noted the time: 10:30 p.m., Monday, August 24. Some joked into their cell phones that they'd come to watch the grass grow. A helicopter hovered overhead. Spotlights zeroed in on the curious scene.

Target Field had grass. Green, green grass. What had been a construction project suddenly became a ballpark. This was as close to a baptism (water was quickly applied) as a baseball stadium can get, and Minnesotans sensed the significance. The Twins publicity team had promoted the installation of grass as a milestone, but who could have anticipated the magnitude of interest?

Local TV crews memorialized the event, then kept returning throughout the week to see how the grass was doing. The story went national, showing up in newspapers from Colorado to Washington, D.C. Traffic on the Twins live webcam shot of Target Field soared from 2,400 views per day to more than 17,000. Two weeks later, a Facebook photo of the grass getting its first clip drew 589 thumbs up and 90 comments within two hours.

Even during the months leading up to the installation, Twins fans had turned up at Graff's Turf Farms in Fort Morgan, Colorado, 50 miles east of Denver, to catch an early glimpse. Apparently, 29 years of "arena baseball" had whetted their appetites for the real game on real grass. Representatives from Major League Baseball told the Twins that they had never seen anything like it. The team reported that several people, while on tours of the new ballpark, were moved to tears at the sight of green grass on the ball field.

It's true that Upper Midwesterners, burdened with months of relentless winter, hold summer sacred. We love open water, green leafy trees, and the feel of soft earth beneath our feet. Our connection to nature during the warmer months is close to mystical. It's why "up north" is so important to us. It's why gardening comes as a reflex. It's why golf is more popular here than anywhere, because of the pent-up anticipation of playing the game outdoors on spongy green grass. The scent of a freshly clipped lawn stirs up all kinds of fond emotions.

Watering the sod at Graff's Turf Farms in Fort Morgan, Colorado

Rolls of sod on their way to the moving trucks

Loading the sod rolls onto the trucks

Upper Midwesterners,

burdened with months

of relentless winter,

hold summer sacred.

The scent of a freshly

clipped lawn stirs up all

kinds of **fond** emotions.

The groundscrew prepares the soil and installs the bases and pitcher's mound in anticipation of the arrival of the sod.

The sod arrives at Target Field.

Feelings about grass ran so strong in August 2009 that a "turf war" broke out. The Minnesota Turf Association complained that the Target Field job should have gone to a local sod farm. "Green with envy" is how the *Star Tribune* described the mood. Even the governor got into the scrap. The Twins explained that this was no ordinary sod but a "system" designed specifically for high-level sports. The team had explored the Minnesota option but concluded that no local vendor could match Graff's experience in supplying the Cubs, Cardinals, Royals, Rockies, Broncos, and Chiefs, as well as college football programs at Notre Dame and Colorado.

A network of tubes below the surface heats the field to keep the grass viable through the winter.

Thirty truckloads were needed to transport the refrigerated sod. Each load took 4 hours to harvest and 14 hours on the road. About 2.5 acres of turf were laid only at night to protect the grass from excessive heat and sun. The job took four nights in all.

The Target Field turf is a thick crop of Kentucky bluegrass. (Bluegrass works best in northern climates, while Bermuda is preferred in southern ballparks.) The grass sits atop a 10-inch layer of soil composed of 93 percent sand and 7 percent peat. The soil, in turn, rests on top of a 4-inch layer of pea gravel. Below that, drainpipes crisscross the field and connect farther below to a cistern that settles and filters the water before discharging it to the storm sewer.

Also beneath the field lies an intricate, 41-mile network of tubes. A mixture of water and glycol, heated by steam from the nearby garbage burner, passes through the tubes to keep the field from falling below 36 degrees in winter. The purpose is not to keep the field consistently warm but to take the sharpest edges off the fierce Minnesota winter and to bring the field gradually into playing condition by the end of March. "Our weather in March is the biggest difference between here and most other major league fields," said Larry DiVito, head groundskeeper at Target Field. It is March that most worries DiVito.

Opposite: Head groundskeeper Larry DiVito waters the Twins' first real-grass playing field since 1981.

THE INNER WORKINGS OF THE TARGET FIELD TURF

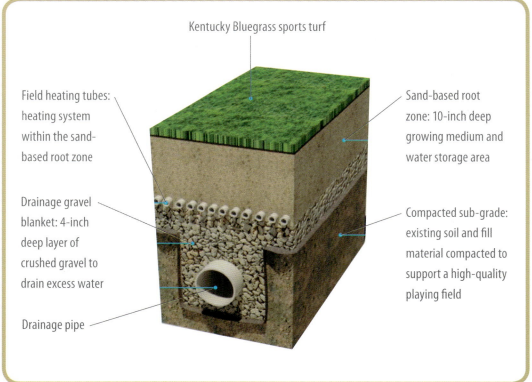

Kentucky Bluegrass sports turf

Field heating tubes: heating system within the sand-based root zone

Sand-based root zone: 10-inch deep growing medium and water storage area

Drainage gravel blanket: 4-inch deep layer of crushed gravel to drain excess water

Compacted sub-grade: existing soil and fill material compacted to support a high-quality playing field

Drainage pipe

LARRY DiVITO Introducing a Team to the Great Outdoors

HEAD GROUNDSKEEPER LARRY DIVITO APPEARS TO HAVE A DEEP AFFECTION for every blade of grass in the Target Field turf. The night the sod arrived from Colorado, he beamed like a new father. This turf was his baby.

Caring for a baseball field is a delicate and difficult thing. The modern groundskeeper is far more than a guy with a water hose and a rake. He's called upon to be a botanist, an agronomist, and a meteorologist—and there's more than a little "art" involved in caring for a field in Minnesota's unpredictable climate. DiVito's 16-hour summer workdays are filled with calculations of air and soil temperature, wind, sun, shade, humidity, soil condition, turf condition, fertilizers, fungicides, and water supply. He must manage crews as well as equipment that includes various hoses, mowers, rakes, and two big tarps. He must consult with the Twins manager and players on how they want the field customized—longer grass for a slower infield, for example, or sloping foul lines to help bunts go fair or foul. And he must talk with umpires about forecasts and rain delays.

During games, DiVito's perch is next to a small, computerized weather station near the visitors' dugout. Radar readings are important, both in deciding whether or not to start a game (the home team's decision) or choosing when to halt play (the head umpire's choice) due to inclement weather.

Before taking over at Target Field, DiVito was head groundskeeper at the Washington Nationals' new ballpark, completed in 2006. He has also been assistant groundskeeper at Dodger Stadium in Los Angeles and, before that, head man for the Boston Red Sox's top farm club in Pawtucket, Rhode Island. A native of the San Francisco Bay Area, DiVito is a baseball man, through and through. He was a graduate assistant coach at Cal Poly and a high school coach in Redwood City, California, all the while building an encyclopedic knowledge of how best to grow grass and groom a field. In Minneapolis, he's also learning about trees, something new for him. Target Field has 138 trees to care for, including 14 black spruces planted in center field and forming a background for hitters.

DiVito is a traditionalist when it comes to field design, preferring simple geometric patterns to the intricate logos that some teams cut into their fields. "We try to present a blank canvas and let the players be the artists," he said. "It's the game itself that's most important. Our job is to make a field that enhances the game. We want to make it fair for both teams."

That said, DiVito knows the baseball custom of cutting logos into the outfield grass and tailoring the field to accentuate the home team's strengths. Under the Dome, the Twins built their success mainly on speed and defense, attributes that were suited to plastic turf and hard-packed dirt. If that strategy changes as the Twins grow accustomed to Target Field, DiVito will be among the first to know. For now, he cuts the grass from 7/8 of an inch to 1-1/8 inch, depending on team desires, and makes other tweaks as requested. He even ponders the color of dirt. The crushed granite on the warning track and the infield mixture is a shade of amber, selected because it goes well with the dark green of the outfield walls. DiVito didn't know when he started that "interior design" would be part of a groundskeeper's job.

For DiVito, a ball field is mostly about green grass and the happy fact that baseball is played on it.

"The question is not whether it's raining at 6:30, but **whether** it's going to be raining at 7, and for how long."

—*Larry DiVito, head groundskeeper*

Larry DiVito gives the Target Field turf its first cut, September 1, 2009.

Larry DiVito

FIELD OF DREAMS

A Tour of Target Field

"Target Field is more than I think anyone,

including myself, could have **imagined**."

—*Joe Mauer, catcher, Minnesota Twins*

The first visit to Target Field is an awe-inspiring—almost dreamlike—experience for fans of all ages.

Twins supporters are thrilled to be cheering for their team in the great outdoors—from the farthest reaches of the outfield upper deck to the prime seats mere feet from home plate.

"This is the fulfillment of a lot of dreams. . . .

[Target Field has] as much **character**,

if not more character, than any ballpark in the country."

—*Bud Selig, Commissioner of Major League Baseball*

After years of dreaming, Twins fans finally have an outdoor ballpark all their own. Target Field is the real thing. From the minute the ballpark opened its doors, people fell in love with the place—its golden limestone and icy glass appendages, the spruce trees in center field, all intended to celebrate Minnesota's natural beauty. The graceful silver canopy overhead brings a touch of urban elegance. Indeed, with its low, prairie-style profile, Target Field seems more a neighbor than a monument.

But most of all, the fans love Target Field because it offers them a chance to see their beloved Twins play under the open skies and on green grass. Some wept at the sight of real grass on the field.

Most everyone has welcomed the park's other friendly features: intimate seating close to the action; great sightlines; wide concourses open to the field and filled with quality food and beverage options; a giant, crystal-clear HD scoreboard loaded with information; a fun and informative celebration of team history; impressive clubhouses that build pride among the players; a fair and lush playing field; sunshine, dramatic sunsets, and all the natural variations that come with an open-air experience—simply put, a classic baseball atmosphere.

"Everything we did in this ballpark we did for a reason," said Jerry Bell, president of Twins Sports Inc. "Notice all the glass we have in here. We wanted to be a part of the city, but you can't be a part of the city unless you can look out and see it."

That vital encounter with the city is perhaps most dramatic at Target Plaza, the first stop on our tour.

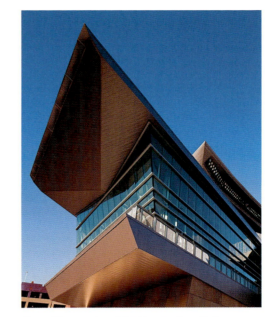

Above: The exterior of the Metropolitan Club and the soaring canopy are icons of dramatic architecture at Target Field.

Below: Aerial view of Target Field, illuminated for the first night game, April 16, 2010

TARGET PLAZA: THE BALLPARK'S "OUTSTRETCHED ARMS"

The best place to meet the ballpark is on Target Plaza, a stylish, 2.5-acre front porch that "floats" over the top of a freeway to form a link between the ballpark and Minneapolis' downtown core. The plaza acts as the ballpark's outstretched arms, extending its main entrances into the heart of the city's entertainment district. Intended as a year-round public gathering place, the plaza's design is a creative blend of contemporary style and traditional baseball imagery.

Nine 40-foot, bat-shaped topiaries form a "lineup" that leads fans to the main gates. Bronze sculptures of the Twins' three Hall of Famers act as a welcoming committee. A Golden Glove sculpture honors the team's Gold Glove winners and offers a prime spot for photos. Benches with visor-shaped sun screens and flower beds the size and shape of pitcher's mounds add to the baseball motif. An undulating 17,000-square-foot wind veil called "The Wave" forms a backdrop to the plaza. The main flag pole is the same one that once overlooked old Metropolitan Stadium. More than 2,000 flowers, shrubs, and trees add natural beauty and texture. Designed by noted Minneapolis landscape architect Tom Oslund, the plaza can appeal to a handful of people seeking serenity or tens of thousands caught up in the thumping excitement of a pennant chase.

The plaza offers a festive, bustling pre-game atmosphere—and lots of opportunities for photos.

Opposite: Featuring art, vendors, and places for relaxation, Target Plaza is both an urban gathering space and the ballpark's main gateway. Fans filing in from Sixth Street cross the plaza to reach Gate 34 (above), the park's primary entrance.

Top: The main flag pole on Target Plaza originally stood at Met Stadium.

Bottom: Two smiling young fans pose on the Golden Glove before the first exhibition game at Target Field on April 2, 2010.

Right: A giant kinetic sculpture, "The Wave," by artist Ned Kahn of Sebastopol, California, forms a backdrop for the plaza.

Kirby Puckett statue

Harmon Killebrew statue

Rod Carew statue

CELEBRATING TRADITION: A HOME OF THEIR OWN

Visitors to Target Field find themselves enveloped in Twins heritage and the history of baseball in Minnesota from the moment they set foot on the ballpark grounds. Almost everywhere hang reminders of past glories and the expectations of glories yet to come.

On the plaza, bronze statues by the acclaimed Minneapolis relief sculptor Bill Mack capture iconic poses from the careers of Hall of Famers Kirby Puckett, Harmon Killebrew, and Rod Carew.

A Tradition Wall lists every player on every Twins team since 1961, rekindling memories of past seasons and past players. Featured along with the familiar heroes are the lesser stars and colorful characters who might have slipped your mind: Jimmie Hall, Jack Kralick, Ted Uhlaender, Bombo Rivera, Scott Stahoviak, and so many others. The display also includes plaques with names of fans and their families. Each donor paid to have family names etched on the wall as a way to pass cherished baseball memories from one generation to the next.

Old Twin Cities ballparks are also remembered on the stylish glass panels of the Minnesota Ballpark History Monument near Gate 29. Colorful banners hanging from the ballpark's exterior walls honor the championships the team has won, as do pennants flying above the left-field stands. The World Series banners (1987 and 1991) are red, the American League pennant (1965) is white, and the division titles (1969, 1970, 2002, 2003, 2004, 2006, and 2009) are blue. The 1987 and 1991 World Series trophies, meanwhile, are on exhibit in the Champions Club.

The Minnesota Ballpark History Monument offers a lesson on the Twin Cities' baseball past. In addition to the Twins' previous ballparks, Met Stadium (1961–1981) and the Metrodome (1982–2009), the monument portrays the old homes of the Minneapolis Millers (Athletic Park, 1889–1896; Nicollet Park, 1896–1955; and Metropolitan Stadium, 1956–1960) and St. Paul Saints (Lexington Park, 1897–1956) of the old American Association.

> "We want both our fans and players to understand that they're all part of a very **special tradition**."

—*Dave St. Peter, president of the Minnesota Twins*

Claiming Target Field as the first "home of their own," the Twins use every nook and cranny to recall the team's rich history. If home is a place to hang family photos, then the ballclub has outdone itself. More than a thousand framed images hang on walls of the ballpark's interior. The team has invested heavily in other artwork, including scores of wall-graphic murals and two huge laser-burned images of Carew and Puckett in the atriums on the Club Level.

Memories are everywhere. Shots of Jim Kaat, Zoilo Versalles, Bob Allison, Don Mincher, Bert Blyleven, Rich Rollins, Camilo Pascual, Vic Power, Gary Gaetti, Tom Brunansky, and many others line the upper concourses. Reproductions of baseball cards, magazine covers, and historic newspaper pages are on display, and famous broadcasting calls from team history are celebrated outside of the press box on the Club Level, including Jack Buck's famous "We'll see you tomorrow night!" from Game Six of the 1991 World Series.

The park aims also to instill in the players a sense of the team's heritage. The first thing players see as they enter the clubhouse area is a large wall graphic with images of past Twins greats accompanied by these words: "tradition, passion, heart, pride, commitment, hustle, team, excellence." The clubhouse itself is loaded with photos, mementos, and other reminders of Twins history.

The team's forebears, the Washington Senators, are not forgotten, and historic photos remind Minnesota fans that their ballclub traces its roots back to the founding of the American League in 1901. Historic photos recall the team's lone World Series triumph in Washington (1924) and depict legendary Senators players like Walter "Big Train" Johnson, Goose Goslin, Bucky Harris, and a young Killebrew. The connections to the nation's capital are also represented by historic photos of Presidents Hoover, Franklin Roosevelt, Truman, and Eisenhower throwing out ceremonial first pitches at Washington's Griffith Stadium.

Other aspects of Minnesota's baseball tradition are highlighted with images of Ted Williams (1938) and Willie Mays (1951) playing for the Minneapolis Millers and Roy Campanella (1948) playing for the St. Paul Saints. Famous native Minnesota ballplayers—including Paul Molitor, Dave Winfield, Roger Maris, Jack Morris, Johnny Blanchard, Terry Steinbach, and Charles "Chief" Bender—are also honored.

Tribute to manager Tom Kelly

Minneapolis Millers Ted Williams and Willie Mays

Famous broadcast calls posted outside the Herb Carneal Press Box

Background: Wood-burned etching of Kirby Puckett, in the Puckett Atrium of the Delta SKY360 Legends Club

POINTS OF VIEW: NOT A BAD SEAT IN THE HOUSE

Great sightlines and unobstructed views give nearly all fans throughout Target Field a clear look at the action, no matter the row or the section. No support pillars get in the way. No need to crane your neck, since all seats face the diamond. Most seats allow spectators to see 100 percent of fair territory—with the exception of a few in the outfield sections, where portions of the warning track and far outfield grass disappear from view. Still, a seat in the highest row of the upper deck in the outfield leaves you closer to the action than a seat in the first row of the upper deck at the Metrodome.

Even if you choose to leave your seat to grab something to eat, use the restroom, or just explore the park, the game will always be in sight. You can walk around the entire Main Concourse without losing sight of the field. And if you take your eyes off the field for a moment, there's likely to be a TV close by; the ballpark has 631 high-definition flat screen monitors.

Among the most popular vantage points are the drink rails placed in several spots around the concourse. They allow fans to catch the action from a variety of angles while mingling with friends, old and new.

The radiant heaters overhead make the drink rails a particularly popular spot during cool evenings.

SEAT OPTIONS

BASEBALL FANS CARE INTENTLY NOT ONLY ABOUT WHERE THEY SIT, BUT HOW THEY SIT. Target Field offers a variety of seat options, all with generous legroom (33 inches). The cream-of-the-crop seating is in the Champions Club, directly behind home plate, where fans sit in luxurious, fully cushioned, high-back chairs. Seats in the Dugout Clubs along the first- and third-base lines have cushioned bottoms, while cushioned seat bottoms with natural wood seat backs lend a North Woods flavor to the Delta SKY360 Legends Club and a small pavilion section in right field. They are the first wood-back seats installed in a major league park since the 1940s. Eighty-two percent of seats in Target Field are individual chairs made of metal and plastic. Traditional bleachers (in the lower section of left field and near the right-field corner) make up just five percent of the total seating, but all bleacher seats have backs for added comfort.

High-back, fully cushioned seat found in the Champions Club and Suites

Plastic-back, bottom-cushioned seat found in the Dugout Clubs

Wood-back, bottom-cushioned seat found in the Legends Club and Pavilion Club

All-plastic seat, found in most sections of the ballpark

The Champions Club offers an up-close perspective and comfortable seating.

MAIN LEVEL

The Main Level at Target Field contains nearly half of the ballpark's seating. The Champions Club, directly behind home plate, offers the most intimate look at the game. You're so close and so low to the field that you can call balls and strikes with the umpire and hear the banter in the dugouts. The Dugout Boxes, which extend down the first- and third-base lines, also offer close-up views—but be sure to stay alert for foul balls!

The Home Plate, Diamond, and Field Boxes fill out the rest of the lower level. Seats on the third-base side offer the ballpark's signature view toward right field and the city skyline in the background.

CLUB LEVEL

The ballpark's second deck comes in two parts. The Town Ball Tavern as well as the popular drink rails and the Skyline Deck are open to all ticket holders. These areas have some of the best views in the park, with the Skyline Deck offering prime vistas of the cityscape. The rest of the Club Level is reserved for luxury seating and dining.

Members of the Delta SKY360 Legends Clubs can choose to watch the game from cushioned outdoor seats or from bar tables and drink rails behind the club's glass walls. The Kirby Puckett and Rod Carew atriums are soaring spaces with fireplaces for members willing to skip an inning or two to enjoy some fine food and drink. Eight Event Suites down the right-field line can be reserved and configured for large or small private parties.

The stylish Metropolitan Club, located in the right-field corner, is open to all season ticket holders. Its outdoor terrace offers food and beverage service along with superb views of the field.

Kids and adults alike can enjoy the game from cozy indoor areas of the Delta SKY360 Legends Club.

Top: Fans at the Club Level enjoy a rich array of amenities along with perfect sightlines.

SUITE LEVEL

Private suites, most of them purchased by corporations, form a third tier at the ballpark. Suite owners and guests can watch the game from outdoor balconies or from luxurious indoor living spaces equipped with flat-screen TVs, bars, and comfortable furniture. With the look and feel of urban condos, these suites have become important financial generators for sports stadiums. Target Field has 54 suites and two mega-suites near the left-field corner; the latter can be rented for large private parties and receptions.

Left: Comfortable outdoor seats offer great viewing of the game from the Suite Level.

Below: The suites at Target Field are like mini-condos, complete with kitchen facilities and high-definition televisions.

Target Field has two bleacher sections: the right-field bleachers are situated near the foul pole, next to the Overlook, and the left-field bleachers (shown here) extend across the lower level from the foul pole to the bullpens.

UPPER DECKS AND OUTFIELD VIEWS

Even fans sitting in the highest levels of the ballpark (the Terrace and View Levels), or in sections farthest from home plate, feel on top of the action. The outfield decks are stacked close to the field to give fans an intimate look. The Overlook section in right, located where Target Plaza meets the ballpark's Main Concourse, juts out over the field and is a prime spot to catch a home run ball. From the Overlook, the angular right-field grandstand sweeps toward the Batter's Eye in center field, just below the Minnie and Paul Celebration Sign. The massive high-definition video board towers above the U.S. Bank Home Run Porch in left. Below the porch is a small bleacher section next to the bullpens.

The Overlook section in right field is prime home-run territory, and the overhanging ledge is one of Target Field's unique features.

Though located in the farthest reaches of the seating bowl, the Batter's Eye section in dead-center and the right-field grandstand are festive places to catch a Twins game.

Flags honoring each of the Twins' World Series, American League pennant, and division championship seasons fly above the U.S. Bank Home Run Porch in the left-field upper deck.

Chef Pastor Jimenez (center) learned cooking from his father, who worked in the kitchens of big hotels in downtown Chicago. The kid worked his way up and eventually found a niche in sports. Jimenez cooked for the Cubs, White Sox, and Bears in Chicago and for the Lakers, Clippers, and Kings in Los Angeles. In 2008, *Sports Illustrated* rated Jimenez's food at Miller Park in Milwaukee the best in baseball.

NOT JUST PEANUTS AND CRACKER JACK: FOOD AND DRINK AT TARGET FIELD

What if you invited 40,000 guests for dinner? What if they came 81 times a year, each with a different hankering, some wanting just peanuts, nachos, maybe a sausage, and a beer or two; others hoping for Caesar salad, sautéed crab cakes, lamb chops with rosemary, pistachio gelato, and a nice Oregon pinot noir?

Pastor Jimenez savors the whole idea. As Target Field's executive chef, he leads a staff of 20 chefs and a hundred cooks who work long hours to deliver a stunning variety of food to the fans. The hot dog still reigns as baseball's number-one delicacy, but the comforts and amenities of today's ballparks have brought premium dining as well.

"We're all about the food," Chef Jimenez says. To him, an excellent grilled hot dog is as noble as an expertly charred filet mignon. "I try to put myself in our customers' shoes. I want to treat people the way I'd like to be treated. That means freshness, flavor, and consistency. And I want to see my food being cooked. I don't want to wonder if it's been sitting around."

Watch food being cooked; then eat it. That's the food philosophy at Target Field. Jimenez calls it "pan to plate," and it's a dictum that holds whether you're at one of the 23 concessions stands on the concourses or in one of the higher-end bars, restaurants, lounges, or clubs. Rather than a central commissary that prepares food for shipment to all corners of the building, Target Field has 20 fully equipped kitchens and dozens of smaller cooking stations. Rarely is food cooked more than a few steps from where it's served. Sausages are rotating on a hot grill. Burgers are constantly sizzling. Chickens and prime ribs of beef are roasting on rotisseries. Salads are tossed before your eyes. And the aromas float out over the crowds and blend in with the baseball atmosphere.

While the concessions stands and vendors offer a steady supply of classic ballpark fare and Minnesota favorites, the menus in the clubs and restaurants change regularly, offering variety with each new visit to the ballpark. "It depends on what's fresh," says Jimenez. "If I call the fish market and they have nice fresh halibut, that's what we'll have."

Delaware North Companies Sportservice manages all the food and apparel concessions at Target Field. Founded in Buffalo, New York, in 1915, the company has been serving major league ballparks since 1930, starting with the Detroit Tigers. "Customers pay high prices for food in ballparks," said Peter Spike, the company's general manager at Target Field. "So it's our job to make sure they're getting high quality."

CLASSIC BALLPARK FARE: HOT DOGS AND BEER

The frankfurter has been a part of baseball's culinary landscape since the 1890s, and still today no other ballpark food stirs so much loyalty and passion. Twins fans had been snarffing down Hormel Dome Dogs by the hundreds of thousands every season since the Metrodome staple was introduced, and people were restless when they learned that Schweigert would be serving up the hot dogs at Target Field. In fact, Schweigert Meats, founded in Minneapolis in 1937, was the maker of the original Twins hot dog at Metropolitan Stadium, and the company has introduced an impressive lineup at the team's new home. The original-recipe Twins Dog, made famous at the Old Met, is the classic. The quarter-pound, all-beef Big Dog replaces the beloved Dome Dog. The Dugout Dog is an old-fashioned sausage with a natural casing, and the Dinger Dog is an extra-long hot dog sold at the Hennepin Grille locations. The Twins expect to sell nearly a million hot dogs in their opening season at Target Field.

The Dugout Dog is sold by vendors toting steam boxes and wearing throwback Schweigert uniforms. The dog is placed on the warmed bun when ordered, not pre-wrapped.

Beer also has a long relationship with baseball parks, and for decades, many teams were associated with local brands. While Anheuser Busch has become baseball's dominant beer provider—and its Bud Light and Michelob Golden Draft are the biggest sellers at Target Field—dozens of different beers are available at the Twins' new home, including a good representation of local brews. Summit, Schells, Grain Belt, Finnegans, and Leinenkugel's are featured at Twins Brews: The Beers of Twins Territory. A total of 14 miles of beer tubes are built into the ballpark fixtures, pumping various brews to 395 taps.

The corn dog—a Minnesota institution

A Kramarczuk sausage, with the works

SIGNATURE DISHES—WITH A MINNESOTA ACCENT

Most new ballparks offer a city's signature dish—cheesesteaks in Philadelphia, barbequed ribs in Kansas City, clam chowder in Boston, crab cakes in Baltimore—and Target Field is no exception. A wide range of Minnesota favorites can be found at restaurants and concessions stands, not least of all at the State Fair Classics stand. Among the favorites are:

- batter-fried walleye on a skewer;
- fresh-roasted corn on the cob;
- Minnesota wild rice chicken soup, from Lunds & Byerlys supermarkets;
- slow-roasted giant turkey leg, a popular item at the Minnesota State Fair and Renaissance Festival;
- Kramarczuk's sausages, including bratwurst, Polish, Italian, and Hungarian, made daily at the popular Eastern European deli in Nordeast Minneapolis;
- Target Field Juicy Lucy, the popular cheese-filled hamburger;
- Angie's Kettle Corn, a sweet-salty favorite from North Mankato.

Some of Minneapolis' finest eateries also get in on the action. The popular Warehouse District restaurant J. D. Hoyt's offers a Pork Chop On-a-Stick; Vincent's on Nicollet Mall reproduces its famed Vincent Burger, premium beef stuffed with smoked Gouda; the Loon Café's Pecos River Red Chili is available both at the ballpark and at the nearby bar-and-grill on First Avenue; and the venerable Murray's Restaurant has supplied the enticing Murray's Steak Sandwich. The landmark barbecue joint Michaelbob's of Naples, Florida—a favorite of the Twins' spring training contingent—imports its Championship Ribs to the great north.

Killebrew Root Beer, named for the Hall of Fame slugger, is a tasty way to quench your thirst, as are a range of Pepsi soft drinks. Caribou, a favorite Twin Cities brand, is the coffee of choice at Target Field.

A wide range of Minnesota **favorites**

can be found at restaurants and concessions stands

throughout the ballpark, not least of all

at the State Fair Classics stand.

Enjoying a Murray's Steak Sandwich

Food is served up hot off the grill at Target Field concessions stands.

Food and drink options abound in Target Field.

CONCESSIONS STANDS

The 23 concessions stands offer a mouth-watering array of ballpark favorites, grilled items, and specialty dishes. Several stands honor memorable figures from Twins history. Halsey's Sausage Haus (brats, hot dogs) memorializes Halsey Hall, the colorful broadcaster from the 1960s and 1970s. Señor Smoke's (tacos, burritos, empanadas) recalls the team's fire-balling reliever Juan Berenguer. Frankie V's Italian (pizza, calzones) honors the stellar left-hander Frank Viola. Tony O's Cuban Sandwiches (roast pork, ham, mustard, and pickles on crusty bread) are sold from mobile carts to honor legendary outfielder Tony Oliva. The State Fair Classics stand offers favorites from the "great Minnesota get-together," including various items on sticks, cheese curds, and more.

Top and right: Hrbek's is often packed with thirsty fans before game time.

Middle: Exterior of the Town Ball Tavern

Bottom: Corridor to the 1st Base Lounge

PUB FOOD GALORE

Restaurants and pubs are plentiful at Target Field. Hrbek's is a classic bar and grill named after Twins legendary first baseman Kent Hrbek. The bar features Twins logos stamped into its tin ceiling and is filled with Hrbek memorabilia. Among its specialties is the monumental Rex Burger, a half-pounder stuffed with melted cheese and caramelized onions. Hrbek's is on the Main Concourse near home plate and offers an outdoor patio.

The Town Ball Tavern on the Club Level is an old-time pub that celebrates Minnesota's deepest baseball roots—the amateur town teams that launched the state's love affair with the game in the nineteenth century. A classic Minnesota bar menu features the walleye sandwich and the Juicy Lucy burger. The tavern's floor is the same one used by the Minneapolis Lakers in their final season (1959–1960).

The Twins Pub is a popular gathering place perched high above home plate on the Upper Level. Beer and classic ballpark food are featured along with live music by organist Sue Nelson.

The 1st and 3rd Base Lounges, tucked away under the stands near each team's dugout, are comfy hideaways that satisfy cravings for traditional ballpark fare and are open to ticket holders in the Dugout Box seating areas. The decor of the lounges celebrates memorable Twins players from each position, including first basemen Vic Power, Don Mincher, and Doug Mientkiewicz and third basemen Rich Rollins, Gary Gaetti, and Corey Koskie.

The Budweiser Roof Deck provides stunning views of the ballpark and the city.

ROOF-TOP VIEWING AND DINING

The Budweiser Roof Deck is a popular party spot offering magnificent views from atop the Twins' administration building in the left-field corner. It also features Major League Baseball's first fire pit. The deck, which accommodates up to 220 revelers in barstool seats and standing room, can be reserved for private parties, but is otherwise open to single-game ticket sales.

The fire pit is a popular hangout on cooler nights.

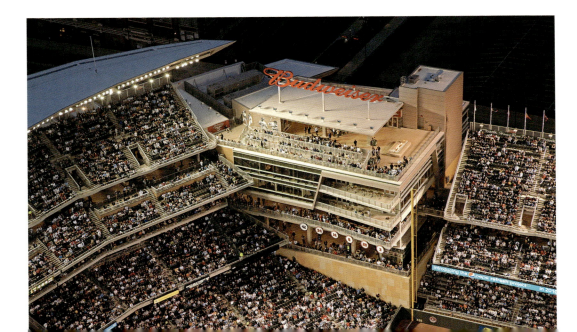

The Champions Club is Target Field's chicest dining spot.

The Rod Carew atrium is one of two spacious lounge areas on the Club Level.

Gourmet food is available in abundance in the Delta SKY360 Legends Club.

FINE DINING IN THE CLUBS

The Champions Club, with its private entrance and cozy atmosphere, is located under the seats behind home plate and adjacent to the Twins' clubhouse. Patrons have a view of the players as they file into the dugout. The dramatic stone walls, fireplaces, leather chairs, and fresh flowers lend elegance to this quiet hideaway. Menus change daily at this most exclusive Target Field restaurant, open only to members.

The Delta SKY360 Legends Club, which wraps around the infield on the second deck, offers several dazzling dining options. Two large atriums, one named for Kirby Puckett and the other for Rod Carew, boast giant wood-etched images of the two Hall of Famers overlooking each dining room. Elegant bars, fireplaces, and huge windows create an atmosphere that evokes a combination of urban style and North Woods comfort. The cuisine ranges from classic ballpark fare to buffets featuring carved roasts, fresh salads, stir-fry dishes, and tempting desserts.

The stylish 573 bar—named to honor Harmon Killebrew's 573 career home runs—offers a quiet retreat for a drink and a sandwich.

The 573 bar celebrates the greatest slugger in Twins history.

The Metropolitan Club combines elegant dining with a strong baseball theme.

The Metropolitan Club reflects the color schemes of the Old Met.

Fans can enjoy the game and some fresh air while partaking in the Met Club's expansive menu.

The Metropolitan Club is one of the most fetching dining spots in the Twin Cities. This soaring, glassy room employs vintage baseball imagery and a color palette that recalls the tiles on Metropolitan Stadium, but its style is sleek and contemporary. With glorious views of both the city and the field from its perch in the right-field corner, the Met Club includes an elevated bar, an outdoor terrace, and an open kitchen that serves up an ever-changing menu of small-plate gourmet delights. The 400-seat restaurant is open to all season ticket holders, although reservations are recommended.

Target Field's dimensions and layout don't require the Twins to change their style of play, but the natural elements can impact the game in this new open-air environment.

The field dimensions at Target Field are nearly identical to those at the Metrodome.

THE FIELD OF PLAY

Target Field's asymmetrical shape reflects its tight urban real estate while closely following the Metrodome's dimensions. Although the left-center power alley at Target Field is eight feet closer and the fence a foot taller, those relatively slight differences by themselves aren't enough to impact the game significantly.

Other factors do come into play, however. Wind, sun, cold, heat, better lighting, real grass, less intense crowd noise, and 27 percent less foul territory have changed the game's dynamics, making the Twins' home field less idiosyncratic and more like other major league layouts.

"I can't wait to see if the piranhas are as good swimming in a new lake," White Sox manager Ozzie Guillen said as he bid farewell to the Metrodome in August 2009. Time will tell whether Target Field will change the Twins' style of play—or their success.

"The Dome was very good to us, but now we're getting back to the basics with playing outdoors," said Twins manager Ron Gardenhire. "We've got our core guys, and we've built our team around those guys no matter which way the field ends up playing. We've got power. We know we can run. All those things come into play no matter what field you're

"We'll see how this new field plays over time. We'll see how the wind blows, and maybe we'll make a few adjustments down the road. But you take our core guys, a Mauer, a Morneau, they're going to do **just fine** no matter what field they're on."

—*Ron Gardenhire, manager, Minnesota Twins*

The spruce trees in the batter's eye and the bright out-of-town scoreboard will take some getting used to for batters and catchers.

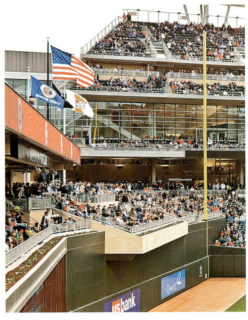

The limestone-faced Overlook juts out over the right field warning track. On a deep fly ball, a right fielder can retreat to the wall, look up to make a catch, and *thud!*—the ball lands in the seats above him for a home run or bounces off the facing for an extra-base hit. It's a quirk that gives Target Field extra personality.

playing on. We'll see how this new field plays over time. We'll see how the wind blows, and maybe we'll make a few adjustments down the road. But you take our core guys, a Mauer, a Morneau, they're going to do just fine no matter what field they're on."

The new ballpark has drawn rave reviews from players, coaches, and managers. Albert Pujols, the first baseman for the St. Louis Cardinals and one of the game's all-time great hitters, praised the ballpark when the Cards came to town for the inaugural exhibition games on April 2 and 3, 2010. "It's a nice place to play," Pujols said. "The infield was unbelievable. I'm pretty sure it'll only get better. There's nothing you can complain about. They did a great job with the design and everything."

Hitters like the dark green backdrop in center field—and will like it even more as the spruce trees grow taller. Infielders compliment the grass and dirt for creating true bounces. They praise the canopy's imbedded lights for not interfering with their vision. Catchers initially complained about the brightness of the out-of-town scoreboard in right-center field, but the Twins have promised to address the problem. Outfielders—and power hitters—are adjusting to swirling and changeable wind currents, but that's nothing new in major league layouts.

The home bullpen at Target Field is completely under cover and has an elevated view of the playing field. Fans sitting at the end of the left-field bleachers, meanwhile, can get up-close views of the pitchers warming up.

DUGOUTS AND BULLPENS

The dugout is a team's nerve center. It's where managers hatch plots, coaches flash signs, and players eat sunflower seeds, spit on the floor, and tell tales that get taller by the day. Target Field's dugouts do nothing to disturb those time-honored rituals, but they do add a touch of elegance to the ballpark's interior. The top of each dugout is clad in a layer of Kasota stone (the same stone that covers the exterior) engraved with the Twins and MLB logos.

The Twins placed the home dugout on the first-base side (a switch from the Metrodome) to allow for a larger adjoining clubhouse. Another change is the mesh fence that runs nearly the length of each dugout to protect players from foul balls.

In the age of specialized pitching, closers and set-up men have become vital to a team's success, making comfortable and convenient bullpens essential to the modern ballpark. As with most newer parks, the bullpens at Target Field are tucked deep into the outfield—in this case, left-center—rather than in foul territory. The two pens for the home and visiting teams are set one in front of the other, with the rear pen elevated. The Twins selected the rear pen because it offers more shade and better views of the game. The proximity to fans tempts the heaping of abuse on opposing relief pitchers, but that has become a ballpark tradition. Target Field's bullpens, by the way, have artificial turf, the only fake grass in the place.

Reliever Jose Mijares gets the call from the bullpen and heads to the mound during Jackie Robinson Day on April 14, 2010.

The Target Field dugouts are spacious and stylish. The fence at field level provides a good perch from which to watch the action—safely behind the mesh.

A pristine dugout before the start of the 2010 home opener.

The dugout during Game 2 of the season.

The elegant digs of the home clubhouse.

The MVP/batting champion/hometown hero gets a coveted corner locker.

"I begged them to let me rehab here so I can be close to

my teammates, and now that's possible because we

have these **wonderful facilities**."

—*Joe Nathan, Minnesota Twins closer, while recovering from elbow surgery*

"Now we're up with the times here in Minnesota. Now we have all the things we

need to really get prepared to play. **It's ours.** We don't have to share it with anybody.

That's important to the mentality of a ballclub."

—Ron Gardenhire, manager, Minnesota Twins

THE CLUBHOUSE

Between 1992 and 2010, more than half of major league teams acquired new ballparks, all with roomy clubhouses that included locker rooms, training and weight rooms, video equipment, and behind-the-dugout batting cages for both the home and visiting teams. It seemed as if the Twins had to go on the road to enjoy the comforts of home.

Having a home you're proud of is a big deal in sports, and the Twins were painstaking in designing their new clubhouse, located beneath the stands on the first base side. "For players, it's our home away from home," said right fielder Michael Cuddyer. "We spend 10, sometimes 12 hours a day here, so you want to make it nice."

In considering the design, general manager Bill Smith visited several other new ballparks to gather ideas. He also sought the opinions of players, coaches, trainers, clubhouse workers, and other staff members.

For the spacious main room, the team decided on an oval-shaped design similar to the one in Philadelphia's Citizens Bank Park. The shape and the absence of pillars were an attempt to promote team unity. "We wanted a room where everyone sees everyone else," Smith said, "and where the manager can walk in and find a player he's looking for."

A thick carpet—adorned with a large Twins logo—covers the floor. Roomy locker stalls made of polished hardwood and equipped with computer plug-ins line the walls. Leather sofas and a half dozen 50-inch flat-screen TVs complete the ensemble, making the space more a plush living room than a locker room. The room is 1,300 square feet larger than the cramped quarters at the Dome.

Directly off the main room are a players' lounge, manager's and coaches' offices, a laundry, showers, a steam room, a large weight room, a doctor's office, an examining room, a training room, and three hydrotherapy pools—one with hot water, one with cold water, and one with a treadmill. There's also a video room for players to study the opposing pitcher and to review their own at-bats.

Smith opted to include most of the home team's amenities in the visiting team's clubhouse as well, although it is slightly smaller. "We wanted to treat them the way we like to be treated," he said, adding that the Twins want all players to like Target Field. "No question it will help us in the free-agent market," he said. "We want facilities that will help us keep our players and lead others to want to play here."

Justin Morneau watches Jason Kubel take his cuts in one of two batting cages located behind the home dugout.

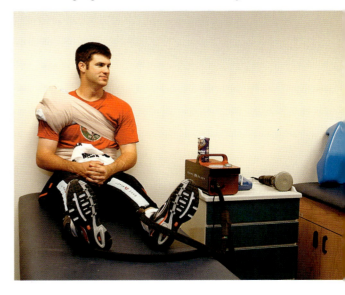

Joe Mauer gets some post-game treatment in the training room.

The broadcast booths at Target Field have clear views of the action.

Media members have some of the best seats in the house.

John Gordon (left) joined the Twins radio team in 1987, and Dan Gladden (right) became his broadcasting partner in 2002. A former left fielder, Gladden keeps a glove handy in case a foul ball comes his way.

COVERING THE GAME: THE PRESS BOX

More than any other American sport, baseball is a daily ritual with a literary bent. Sometimes it's hard to tell which is more glorious, the game itself or the retelling of it. Hacks, poets, and golden-voiced broadcasters have occupied baseball press boxes over the years. The box at Target Field is named in memory of Herb Carneal, the affable man with the mellow Virginia drawl who served as the Twins' radio voice for 45 years until his death in 2007.

Initial plans had the press box perched high in the upper deck, clinging to the canopy. It was shifted to the Club Level to give reporters a closer look at the field and to improve ballpark aesthetics. The roomy, tri-level box can accommodate 90 writers and statisticians as well as home, visiting, and national broadcast crews. There's also a room for press conferences on the Event Level near the home and visitors clubhouses.

The Twins wanted to ensure that the ballpark's distinctive good looks would come across on television broadcasts, making it instantly recognizable around the country. The main clues: the golden limestone, the Minnesota-shaped Minnie and Paul Celebration Sign above the grove of spruce trees in center field, the dramatic angles of the canopy, and the views of the Minneapolis skyline. "No doubt we're in the land of ten thousand lakes," said ESPN's Bobby Valentine. "This place looks like Minnesota."

The spacious press box allows members of the media to keep a close eye on the game as they write their stories. The front of the box can be fitted with glass panels to protect the reporters from inclement weather.

"I **appreciate** that the Twins asked for our advice in designing the press box. I think they batted almost a thousand."

—La Velle E. Neal III, baseball beat writer, Star Tribune

BERT BLYLEVEN

SID HARTMAN

Bert Blyleven has been a part of the Twins family for nearly 15 years as a broadcaster and more than a decade as a Twins player. Minnesota native Dick Bremer (in the background) has been the play-by-play man on television since 1983.

BERT BLYLEVEN, THE COLOR COMMENTATOR for Twins television broadcasts on Fox Sports North, had a steller 22-year major league career pitching for the Twins, Rangers, Pirates, Indians, and Angels. He made his debut as a 19-year-old with the Twins and spent his first six and a half seasons with Met Stadium as his home ballpark. He returned to the Twins in 1986, just in time to contribute to the team's World Series championship season at the Metrodome in 1987. After retiring in 1992, he joined Dick Bremer in the Twins' TV booth in 1996, lending his tart sense of humor to the broadcasts. Never a big fan of the Metrodome, Blyleven loves the airy views and close-to-the-action vantage point that Target Field provides. "It's a beautiful view from where we're at," he said. "We don't have this beam over our heads, so we can actually see fly balls. We have a beautiful view of downtown, especially at night, and a great view of the scoreboard. It's all first class. It's as good or better than anywhere we broadcast in baseball."

SID HARTMAN HAD BEEN WRITING newspaper columns for 65 years when Target Field opened in 2010, and the 90-year-old journalist was thrilled to be prowling the new dugouts and locker rooms in search of a great story. "It's fantastic," he said of the new digs. "The press box, this time they built it big enough so that when they get the All-Star Game or the World Series they can handle everybody. You've got to give the Pohlads credit for this whole thing. They put in a lot of extra money to make it first class. It's like you're building a house and your wife says, 'Honey, if we added a room it would be a much better house.' They came through and Target came through and made this a first-class place. It's as nice as any ballpark anywhere."

PRESENTING THE GAME

Good road signs guide your trip without cluttering up the scenery. The same holds for a good baseball experience. A good scoreboard adds valuable information without distracting from the action on the field. A good public-address announcer keeps fans up to date without upstaging the players. Good music enhances the atmosphere without drowning out the sounds of the game itself.

It's a delicate balance. The Twins aim to achieve a classic baseball atmosphere at Target Field—but with some impressive, state-of-the-art digital touches. The immense video board and remarkable sound system have the potential to dazzle a crowd, and the challenge comes in knowing when to use the technology and when to step back. "We want to get away from bombarding the fans," says Andy Price, director of broadcasting and game presentation.

Price heads a staff of 35 people, and during games, most of them are stationed in a large control room on the upper deck overlooking the first-base line. Except for the spontaneous addition of rally music, each game is scripted from start to finish, like a major television program. The script is typically finished well before the first pitch, giving technicians enough time to practice their moves. A director punches buttons on a giant console while a producer selects camera shots, reconfigures the scoreboard, barks directions to the various digital-board operators, and cues the PA announcer, the organist, and the mascot. "We're everything that happens," Price said, "except the baseball."

THE VOICE OF TARGET FIELD: Adam Abrams

ADAM ABRAMS IS THE MAN BEHIND THE MICROPHONE for baseball-related announcements at Target Field. It has been tough for Abrams to replace his friend and mentor, the legendary Bob Casey, who died in 2005. But Abrams brings his own style and insights. "I try to be informative and professional. I don't try to be the show," he said. "The game is the show. It's almost better if people don't notice me so much. I do try to give the players' names an extra zip when it's called for, especially in introducing the starting lineups, and in the bottom of the ninth if we need a little more energy. But outdoors means a more relaxed atmosphere. At Target Field I'm a little more conversational and a little less in your face."

The control room at Target Field

The Twins aim to achieve a **classic** baseball atmosphere

at Target Field—but with some impressive,

state-of-the-art digital touches.

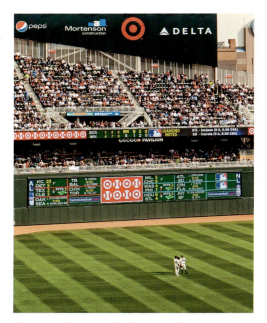

Above: In right-center field, the out-of-town scoreboard and "Diamond Notes" keep fans abreast of action around the major leagues.

Right: More than any feature, the 46-foot-tall Minnie and Paul Celebration Sign in center field brands Target Field as the home of the Twins. The cartoon figures, revived from the team's first logo, show the Twin Cities shaking hands across the Mississippi River. The neon sign lights up—and the characters actually do shake hands—when a Twins player hits a home run.

Opposite: Target Field's HD video board is the fourth largest in the majors.

THE SCOREBOARD

Target Field's main video board in left field is the fourth largest in baseball, measuring nearly six stories tall by ten stories wide—that's nine times larger than the scoreboard at the Metrodome, or as big as 1,042 42-inch TV monitors. The board's 4.4 trillion shades of color, 1,080 lines of resolution, and 4.8 miles of wiring give "high definition" a whole new meaning. Instant replays are so crystal-clear that you can tell if a player shaved before the game.

There is an impressive volume of information for the fan to take in. The main board pumps out at least 50 pieces of data during each at bat: the player's photo, his hometown, his height and weight, his up-to-the-minute hitting stats, the results of his previous at bats, his performance with the bases loaded (if they're loaded), and so on. And then there's the line score, the balls-and-strikes count, and the Twins-O-Gram—a returning relic from the old Met that presents special messages and announces the community groups at the ballgame.

The electronic ribbon board at the base of the Home Run Porch in left field informs fans of the results of the previous play, the speed of the last pitch, the pitcher's game stats, and the line score. Another board just above the bullpen gives the pitcher's real-time season stats and notes who's warming up. The out-of-town scoreboard embedded in the right-field wall shows real-time information on as many as fourteen other games. Another ribbon board above the Powerball Pavilion in right field provides notes from around the majors.

THAT'S ENTERTAINMENT

According to Sue Nelson, organ music is "the sound of baseball."

Mascot T.C. loves to ham it up (no pun intended) for the crowds.

SUE NELSON'S ORGAN MUSIC: THE SOUNDS OF BASEBALL

Years ago, the Twins' effervescent organist Sue Nelson played in piano bars. Now, at Target Field, she's back at it. Her 1970s vintage Yamaha—a veteran of Met Stadium and the Dome—is located in the Twins Pub high above home plate. Surrounded by fans drinking and having a good time, Sue belts out old favorites (like "Talkin' Baseball") as well as rally music ("Here we go, Twi-ins, here we go!"). With all the people around, it's harder for the chatty organist to concentrate on the game, but she loves the vibrant atmosphere. "Coming in here is like a dream," she said. "So many people thought it wouldn't happen, and now we're here!"

T.C. THE MASCOT

He doesn't slide into a tank of beer like Bernie Brewer in Milwaukee, or torment opponents like the Phillie Phanatic, or dance quite like the San Diego Chicken. T.C., the Twins mascot since 2000, is more like an ambassador of Minnesota Nice. He hugs kids, poses for photos, shoots t-shirts into the stands, and when not entertaining fans at Target Field, visits schools and hospitals and marches in parades. T.C. is a cuddly cheerleader and a big part of the team's family-friendly appeal. Older fans note T.C.'s resemblance to his ancestor, the lovable Hamm's Bear, a popular cartoon figure "from the land of sky blue waters," featured in Hamm's beer commercials of the 1950s and 1960s.

SHOPPING AT TARGET FIELD

Anyone for stocking caps? Umbrellas? Sunscreen? Twins fans need to stock up for outdoor baseball, and Target Field's gift shops and souvenir stands have everything they might need to keep warm, dry, and unburned—while also displaying their allegiance to the home team.

The spacious 4,600-square-foot Twins-Majestic Clubhouse Store, located next to Gate 29 in right field, sells a breadth of team gear—everything from T.C. earrings to bumper stickers, key chains, and a huge selection of apparel for men, women, and children. Aside from the main store, a New Era cap shop is located down the left-field line, and three satellite Twins Gear stores can be found on the Main Concourse and on the Club and Suite Levels.

Fans decked out in full Twins regalia consider more items at the Twins-Majestic Clubhouse Store.

A young fan tries on one of the many Twins caps available at the ballpark store in a variety of colors, styles, and logos.

Souvenir stands throughout the ballpark and on Target Plaza offer ample opportunity to stock up on Twins gear.

A fireworks display signals the conclusion of another Twins victory—but it's going to be a while before Target Field goes to sleep for the night.

SHUTTING DOWN FOR THE NIGHT

The game isn't really over when it's over. The stands need to be swept clean, the field watered, the infield raked, the floors mopped, the uniforms washed, the newspaper reports filed, the dishes put away, the scoreboard shut down. After all of that, the lights are turned off, the parking lots empty out, the bells clang, and the last train departs. Until the game tomorrow.

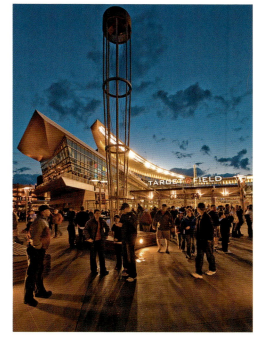

Even after the game ends, people don't seem to be in any hurry to leave Target Field, stopping to take pictures on the plaza and sharing the experience with fellow fans.

"This place is so **nice**,

people don't want to leave."

—*Scott Seeker, ticket taker, Target Field*

The Hiawatha light-rail line is just one of several convenient ways for fans to get home after the game.

AFTERWORD

by Joe Mauer

AS A KID GROWING UP IN ST. PAUL, I remember the excitement of getting ready to go to a Twins game. Playing baseball all summer, I could only attend a few games each year, so each one was a special event. But what I remember most is heading to the ballpark in my T-shirt and shorts on a beautiful summer day and then having to go inside. At the time, it didn't really matter to me. When you're young, you're just pumped to go to a big league baseball game.

The first time that I actually saw a major league game outdoors, I was playing in one for the Twins. Over the years, I have seen Twins fans make the trips to Milwaukee, Kansas City, and Chicago, where they could enjoy what it was like to be outside and watch a baseball game. You would see how much they enjoyed the atmosphere, and you could tell they'd wanted it for a long time here in Minnesota.

And Target Field is more than I think anyone, including myself, could have imagined.

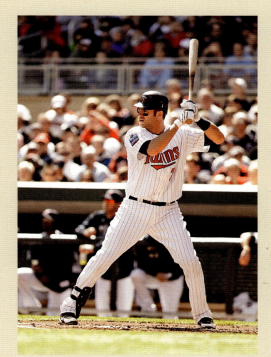

It's hard to put into words what this new ballpark means to me. I know our team—my teammates and our coaching staff—they are definitely appreciative of it, and I think they have a good idea of how long the people here in Minnesota have been waiting for something like this. Being from here and living it, it hits me a little more.

When I ran out on the field before the first exhibition game, as I always do to go warm up a pitcher, the reception I got was almost like getting the game-winning hit. You could just feel the excitement in the air—the fans are excited about Twins baseball. They are excited to see us out on the field and playing outside. There were a lot of smiles up in the stands during that first home stand, and the crowd even cheered when the rain fell during our second game here. That was the first time I've ever heard a crowd cheering for rain.

The first thing I noticed when I walked into Target Field was the attention to detail. When you walked into the Metrodome, everything was kind of bland. It didn't really say Twins or Minnesota or anything like that. But now when you walk on the field as a player, you see the spruce trees in center field and the limestone. It definitely looks like a Minnesota ballpark.

Then there are the touches inside the clubhouse. One of the biggest things that hit me when I walked in were the quotes on the wall from Kirby Puckett ("Live for today. Tomorrow isn't promised to anyone.") and Tom Kelly ("We're all in this boat together. Everybody grab an oar."). Those are the things that Gardy and people throughout the organization talk about all the time. So to have those little reminders is pretty neat.

It hasn't quite sunk in yet that this will be our home for many years to come. But having Target Field means the Twins will be here for a long time. It's the team that I always cheered for, and to think that millions of our fans will get to call Target Field home is pretty special.

ACKNOWLEDGMENTS

I wish to thank people who in many and various ways contributed abundantly to this book, especially: Dave St. Peter, Josh Leventhal, Molly Gallatin, Kevin Smith, Katie Sonmor, Cindy Samargia Laun, Jerry Bell, Dan Mehls, Eric Curry, Kim Kaisler, Dave Mansell, Bruce Miller, Earl Santee, and Kelly Thesier.
—Steve Berg

The Twins organization would like to thank the many individuals and organizations who made Target Field a reality: primary project founders such as the Pohlad family and Hennepin County; critical project partners such as the Minnesota Ballpark Authority, the City of Minneapolis, the Minnesota Department of Transportation, the Metropolitan Council, and Target Corporation; the talented and creative project team led by Mortenson Construction and Populous; the 3,500-plus skilled men and women who safely worked together to construct this beautiful ballpark; and the millions of Twins fans who have long awaited a day to call this ballpark home. Thank you for your leadership, vision, ingenuity, passion, and support.

PHOTO CREDITS